TEACHING
behind the WIRE

MY TEACHING EXPERIENCE IN A
CALIFORNIA MAXIMUM PRISON

STANLEY LOCKSHIN

PAGE PUBLISHING, INC.
New York, NY

First originally published by Page Publishing, Inc. 2018

ISBN 978-1-64462-414-2 (Paperback)
ISBN 978-1-64462-415-9 (Digital)

Printed in the United States of America

This book is dedicated to the memory of Stanley Lockshin who passed before he saw the dream of his story in print.

December 27, 2018

Dear Rona,

During the last several days a number of Stan's former students approached me and offered their condolences over the loss of a man who touched so many lives. Many of the inmates who are enrolled or have completed college programs had their first success in Stan's GED class. His enthusiasm and love of learning made his class a magnet for many who had never known any success in school. I had the great pleasure to teach in the classroom next to his and often watched him at work. He made history come alive and wove it into nearly every lesson. His students always excelled in math and he knew every students weak area and how to focus on what they needed. Stan had a special gift that he shared with all his students and he loved to brag deservedly over their achievements when the GED test results were announced.

Stan was also a champion for school improvement and raised a few administrators' eyebrows for not providing the support he felt was needed for continuing school improvement. All of the staff admired him for his uncompromising viewpoint that was always student centered.

For all of us who were his friend and mentor he will be truly missed. He will remain in our hearts and memory for the great work he did and the time we shared with him. I hope I was able to touch on a few things that made this man so special and admired.

Larry Wehr

⊛NOW HEAR THIS⊛

December 14, 2018

18-033

Passing of Retired Teacher Stanley Lockshin

It is with deepest sorrow California State Prison, Los Angeles County (LAC) announces the passing of retired Teacher Stanley Lockshin on December 10, 2018.

Mr. Lockshin began his career with the California Department of Corrections and Rehabilitation as a teacher on May 12, 1997. He retired on August 9, 2012. Mr. Locksin will truly be missed by all his family and friends at LAC. Our sincerest condolences are extended to his family, friends, and loved ones during this difficult time.

R.C. JOHNSON
Warden (A)
California State Prison -- Los Angeles County

Preface

T his assessment and book started with my master's dissertation while working as a teacher in the California prison system. The master's program was for administration as supervision, with Tier 1 credential administration. The purpose of this book is designed as an individual study of working in such a system and institution.

Some people who read this material will find it difficult to believe; some colleagues may or may not agree on what is within the pages. The main purpose is to provide information and allow the reader to come to their own conclusion.

I have taught in the California prison system for the last seventeen years as an educator. I can attest that my abilities have kept me sane and going for that time. At times, I have wondered who the keepers were and who the inmates were, since there is a fine line of distinction between the two. Family and friends have asked, "How can you teach there, and is what you do really teaching?" The answer for me is obvious. I chose to teach in a state prison after a twenty-five-year career in sales. I received my teaching credential in 1974. I was a substitute teacher in East and South Central Los Angeles. In 1975, the district wanted minority teachers, which I was not. My wife was pregnant. I needed gainful employment. I went into the sales arena and stayed there for over a quarter of a century.

However, my wife believed that my destiny was teaching, and in 1996 I would return to that profession. Like anywhere else, teaching for the state is not a career in which to become wealthy, nor was it my reason for changing careers at the age of forty-seven. In November 2005, I suffered an injury at work that resulted in a major back surgery in August 2006. During this downtime, I began writing this book.

I would like to thank my wife, Rhona, of forty-three years for her support; I leave the rest to you. I hope you find what I have written to be of interest to you.

—Stan Lockshin

Prologue

On August 10, 2012, I retired from the California Department of Corrections, and with my service as a GED teacher at Lancaster State Prison, you might ask why I've written this now almost three years later. There are two reasons.

The first reason is getting all my material in order: writing longhand and typing it, having people read said typing and edit. Everyone is a yenta, and that's okay. I found it helpful, the suggestions useful and important. Also, I added more information.

The second reason was that from October 14, 2014, to 12/18/2015 I went through five surgeries. In one of them, I had no use of my hands. It's very difficult to use your hands when they look like a cloud. Hard to write, eat, or take care of bodily functions. By September 2015, with therapy I had regained 90 percent use of my hands, especially the feeling in my fingers.

This work is totally based on my experiences. Friends who readied my material told me I was too specific; like a sense of humor, sarcasm kept my mind and myself going for a very long time. I could and did compare it to "mash," where those have appeared to have lost their minds to keep their sanity. The same application applied to me.

In doing this updated prologue, people had asked me if I had seen the HBO Special "toe tag people" about Lancaster State Prison and the horror yard: where all the inmate interviews came from.

I did watch that show. I knew "a yard," the horror yard, for the eight years I taught there. I knew of the inmates who were interviewed—for years—and like myself had grown older.

For those of you who don't know "toe tags," they are the identification card attached to a body's big toe for identification purposes: it does not matter which one. The idea is that those inmates who have a life without a parole sentence consider this to be the "new death penalty," and "toe tag parole" infers that the inmate is paroled after he is dead.

These inmates who were interviewed truly believe that a life sentence in most European countries should be twenty-five years, period. I heard these conversations, with many of them I would agree or on a case-by-case method. All the inmates knew I was a death penalty advocate, still am, and that everyone has the right to an opinion. I knew many inmates who had completed thirty years or more. Are they the same person who committed a capital crime at eighteen or twenty and are now over fifty years old?

For this inmate who has committed a capital offense, it is rational for them to say "I've served thirty years, I'm not the same." What about redemption? I can say when I first started my career I read many inmates' files and was appalled at what they had done. It would not have been smart to say "I know you're a killer!" to anyone there.

The inmates don't talk about what they have done or why they are in prison. It's never discussed, ever. I never brought up this issue, even when I was told by one who gave me a brief description of what he was incarcerated for. He believed every word he told me—it was all a lie. I had read his file.

Prison advocate groups are always screaming about "prisoners' rights." What about the rights of the victims? Oh, I forgot—most are dead and unremembered. Many people remember Charles Manson and his life sentence for murder, but how many people remember the names of people killed by him and his associates? (Hint—Sharon Tate.)

This entire program on HBO was to create sympathy for these inmates and perhaps create a second chance for them.

Introduction

"What the hell am I getting into?" I said to myself on my first day on May 10, 1996, as I walked into the prison and toward what would become my classroom and students. I was originally a long-term teacher in East Los Angeles, and following that, I had then spent the last twenty-five years in sales and was getting tired of it. At the tender age of forty-six, my wife asked me what I wanted to be when I grow up. I decided to go back to teaching. I taught at the same prison until I retired on August 10, 2012. Lancaster State Prison is a maximum security facility, with four yards (A–D) as well as a minimum yard for those inmates who have less than a year to serve. Each yard is run like a kingdom with each yard captain acting as king.

I taught GED throughout the institution and realized very quickly that this institution had a unique "food chain" (i.e. custody, top rank; free staff, noncustody; and lastly, the inmates). I worked in classrooms where you fried in the summer and froze in the winter. The air-conditioning wouldn't work in July, but in January the temperature in a classroom could drop to forty degrees. As a teacher, I was "free staff" and considered less than zero. If you were noncustody you were invisible. However, the only time we came visible was when there was a lockdown of inmates. On one occasion in the C Yard, the inmates were locked down for four months, and we teachers had to work in the kitchen preparing breakfast and lunch for twelve hundred inmates. We never saw staff from any other department through our "dark age." We went through a period of misery brought on by poor management, the topic of which I discuss this later in the book.

By 2012, I was burned out and given the following choices: A—have a stroke; B—punch someone out; or C—retire. I chose to retire. Timing is everything.

I hope you enjoy what I have written as "truth is stranger than fiction" and none of this has been made up. All the content of this book is true.

The GED

T he GED is a double-edged sword, and I will tell you why. As a GED teacher, it was important to me to have many students pass the test: (1) for their own accomplishment and (2) to either attend vocational programs or get an AA degree. This program was and is beneficial because it places a certain percentage of inmates in a classroom for six hours a day. These are six hours that they are not in the yard where they might create mischief.

Of course, the GED graduation is great as it allows parents, family, friends, and news media the opportunity to see the success of these persons. There is nothing like success and a graduation to make people "warm and fuzzy" on the inside. This is powerful. However, now that I'm retired, it is my belief and opinion that part of the GED is a scam, and let me explain my rationale.

In the real world, our world, a person with a GED has the ability to move upward educationally (the inmate also), but there's the catch. The inmate, when paroled, has the ability to seek employment from a business. The inmate without parole has nowhere to go. I've known a good many inmates who have their GED, four or five AA degrees, and are going to be in prison forever. Management was and still is tickled pink they can show these wonderful results. Yes, it shows that the inmate has made progress for when he goes to his parole hearing, if he has one. Lifers may have hearings, but that is just "pro forma."

The prison system uses the classroom as a dumping ground. I've had inmates in my GED class who had their GED, a BA, an AA degree, or had a master's degree. Some could barely read or write. I thought it particularly funny when some were so heavily medicated that they didn't know where they were, who they were, who I was, or why they were in the class. I laughed when an eighty-year-old inmate was assigned to my class so that on his tombstone it would not only give his name and birth-death dates, but also it would say, "Got GED!"

It was hard to understand why any inmate who didn't have a parole date was eligible to take this test. Perhaps it's the system's quota of twenty students per teacher, but the concern was that we were wasting time, money, and manpower. Staff requested management to attempt to be more selective with the GED to the inmates that would stand to gain the most benefit. This procedure happened many times and was stopped when too many teachers were injured, and the union grew some balls and put its foot down. That was the end of us working in the kitchen.

The prison did not have a good reputation. Of thirty-two prisons in California, it ranked thirty-second. Being on the bottom, we have the ability to move up in ranking. It bounced around like a cork in a bottle in a pond. Our managers were happy that our paperwork for the end of the month was perfect. Many people who transferred from other institutions hated working here. However, they also loved it because Lancaster was a "cash cow," offering plenty of overtime for those who sought it. One teacher who had been an artist teaching basic education had the inmates do cartoons all day. Another gave worksheets and read the *L.A. Times* all day for ten consecutive years—not a good way for your tax dollars to work.

I will not use any real names in this book except for one: my dear friend Tom Miguel who was our principal for many years. I met Tom in 1996 as a supervisor of vocation training. He retired as a chief deputy warden and was a man of impeccable character, a great leader. During his time as principal, we went through a "golden age." He was extremely devoted in the way the school operated and was able to get 110 percent out of the department. Alas, after he was transferred in 2004, we went into the real world.

Is this program a numbers game to pacify the powers in Sacramento?

The Giant Enema

During the period of our last recession, the home sale market blew up. The state was losing billions in revenue and billions in debt, requiring that major changes be made throughout the state. This lasted almost three years.

To save money, the first agenda Sacramento decided was that those employed by the state would lose 5 percent of their pay (note: this would eventually peak at 15 percent). The employees were given one to two days off, usually on Friday without pay. The next and most difficult blow was the reduction of all vocation/educational staff across the state. Education took a harder hit than any other department across the state, losing about 75 percent of the existing workforce; those that reached retirement age retired. All these reductions in staff were based on seniority. For instance, if a teacher had less than five years of state service, they were gone. The greater the length of seniority, the greater the chances you had of being "bumped" by someone else from another institution. At our prison, there was total chaos. Teachers were feeding on daily rumors—kissing the principal's ass and turning on each other. I know people who were pissed off at me because I had fifteen years of seniority at the time and would not be cut. Teachers with less than five years of service would either be cut or placed on priority basis for any job opening other than teaching. My two friends Gayle and Val went from $65,000 per year to $35,000 per year. Both had their homes foreclosed because they were unable to pay the mortgage.

The irony of the story is this: most of the people I know in custody couldn't have cared less about their fellow employees getting the chop. Their attitude simply amazed me. This noncaring attitude was also common among other noncustody staff. However, as of 2014, both Gayle and Val have returned to full-time positions in the department.

In-Service Training

With most professions such as doctors, lawyers, financial planners, and others, these individuals are required to attend by class or self-study material continuing education courses to keep themselves up to date in their chosen profession. They are to log, by law, a given number of clock hours per year or every other year to keep licenses in place. For example, we teachers have to have our credentials renewed every five years and show proof of classes and lectures taken to complete the amount of clock hours required.

The Department of Corrections has a mandate that all employees attend in-service training. During the year, there are classes for correctional officers and for all other staff. Some of these classes overlap, and the classes have people in them from all departments at the end of each class, which can be from one to two hours. Tests are given, and the persons taking the test signs a document that he/she had completed the class. Usually eighty to one hundred hours are the requirement. This information is kept on computer, and at the end of the year, employees are given a memo that says they have completed the hours for the year, or they don't have enough and have to catch up. The standard courses are given every year such as those on inmate escape, riots, and medical and general procedures.

One of the classes that is given every year is called "Anatomy of a Setup." To be brief, it's about how an inmate will use an employee for certain favors. Perhaps, giving the inmate candy, gum, or magazines—just little favors. Then the inmate reels you in. He wants another contraband: drugs, money, smokes—whatever, and if you say no, he will turn you in, and now you belong to him until he squeezes you dry and then turns you in. Not a pretty picture.

Everyone says, "That won't ever happen to me!" Really? Every year at this facility, six to ten people were "walked out." They were either prosecuted or given prison sentences because they were too smart and would never get caught. Greed is a terrible thing. Staff would get caught up in this from one year on the job to over twenty years employed. In all the years I worked there, I personally knew at least twenty people who had compromised their job for greed.

I found all the classes interesting, and the information was extremely important in keeping us safe and secure, including myself. Where I may have been a pain to some people, I was actually attentive in keeping myself from harm by paying attention to these classes. Yes, we had the same ones year in and year out, and they were important to know and follow. They kept you out of harm's way and alive. The classes that most of us liked were the medical ones.

Our senior nurse taught classes on blood-borne pathogens, what to touch and what not to in case of inmate injury (with all the diseases we had, I was certainly not going to touch anything!). We had inmates with HIV and hepatitis C. So if an inmate was stabbed in my area or had bled on me, I had to go to the infirmary to be checked out. As a fairly new teacher at the beginning of my career, I was "gassed." What this means is that an inmate throws urine, feces, or blood on you. In my case, it was urine, but I still had to be checked out in the infirmary.

During one medical class, we were told that a certain racial group was having many members sent to the hospital. It seems that to prove their manhood these inmates had taken round pebbles or marbles and sewn this material into the heads of their penises. Unhappily, they had not used the most sterile material to do this. They used what was at hand, such as dental floss and thread from their blankets to do the sewing.

The senior nurse would tell us this information right before lunch or how the medical staff had to surgically undo what had been done. This worth RN went into great detail on telling us about pus, corruption, and damage to male members. He told these stories with great gusto and, at the end of telling them, asked if we were ready for lunch.

The medical department was always great in getting us good information.

SGT Bilko and the Inmate Veterans

I sponsored several programs, one for inmates who had served in the military. The reason I started this selection with SGT BILKO is because there was a TV show, for those of you who are baby boomers, in the 1950s about an sergeant who was the ultimate scrounger in the army. I could relate to him as I, too, was the ultimate scrounger during my four years in the Air Force and carried over to my career with corrections.

I was asked by an inmate who was a Native American named Young Bull, an army veteran who was serving a life sentence, if I would be the sponsor for the inmate vets.

Their previous sponsor, also one of our teachers, had told these vets that he was a retired navy seal who could kill a person with a sheet of paper. This sponsor who was a modest 450 pounds would tell these vets how he had singularly won the Vietnam War. These gentlemen learned quickly that he was a bullshit artist, had him removed as a sponsor, and the program had lain dormant for about eight months. The reason the inmates asked me to be the sponsor was that I was honest, was a "Nam" vest, and most of all, not a bullshit artist.

The first order of business was to create an acceptable proposal that the warden could support and sign off on. As in every bureaucracy, it had to go through a chain of command from lieutenant to captain of a yard to the assistant warden to the associate warden, and finally, the warden. My three-page proposal of one hundred pages came back to me the size of the novel *War and Peace*. Below is a sample of some of the questions that were asked:

1. When, when, and what time would we meet?
2. Would this program interfere with any other program on the yard?
3. Would inmates be pulled from jobs they had?
4. Would overtime be required for officers, and would they be pulled from other duties?
5. Inmate veterans had to be discipline-free (no written charges) for five years.
6. Number of veterans involved.

These were just a few of the questions that had to be ensured.

It was decided that twenty inmates would be in this group. Young Bull would provide a list of all the vets on a yard, and we would do a screening to get our group together. Some of the inmate trustees have held their positions for a very long time and, after a while, have come to believe that prison employees work for them and not the other way around.

An example of this is that he provided me with two candidates that I found questionable. The first candidate had a Russian name—no big deal—but when I asked him what branch he had served in, to my surprise he responded that he had served as a commando in the Russian Army. I removed him from our list over Young Bull saying, "He was in the army," and I replied, "The Russian Army and he's out!"

The second candidate, who I had removed from the group, was not a US Military veteran, but his wife was. Young Bull and I had almost a similar discussion when I told him this inmate was not a vet and not a candidate for our group. Needless to say that Young Bull was highly annoyed. I told him I was the sponsor, not he, and we do things my way, not his, and that he would be removed from his trusteeship with me and work for someone else with a negative recommendation to hire him. He saw the light, and we did things my way.

Our group would meet every Friday from one thirty to two forty-five when inmates had returned to their cells. My classroom was the area of our round-robin talks. Branches of the service are

Vietnam vets from all branches of the service. I did not inquire what sent them to prison. It was not my business. What we talked about was where we served and what we did. I was also able to provide information for them or what the VA could provide while in prison and when paroled. We used books, movies, and guest speakers who had also served in the military. I worked with this group for about six months before I retired. Still, it is going strong.

PS: Before my retirement, I was asked to be the sponsor for the Native Americans as a Jewish boy from Brooklyn, New York. I didn't know whether they were serious or pulling my leg.

Lt. Commando and I

L t. Commando and I started working at the prison in May 1996: he as a corrections officer and I as a teacher. As fate would have it, we were assigned to the C ward, which was commonly known as Jurassic Park! Every day was the Fourth of July: stabbing, inmates being shot during rioting, and all kinds of mayhem. He was known to one and all as Officer Commando.

The reason for this name, which I gave him, was due to the fact that if there was any disturbance on the yard, no matter how large or small, one would find him in the midst of the action. No matter where the action was on the yard, if he had to run two hundred yards to involve himself in any activity or altercation, he would; he was a hard charger. He was very self-centered and wrapped up in his own importance. There was no problem when he did a job, but then he could become a pain in the ass. We did not get along.

When he became a sergeant, he was insufferable. He believed that we teachers did not belong; inmates were not worth being educated and should be kept in their cells twenty-four hours a day and were a waste of taxpayers' dollars. I had a classroom of twenty-eight students, and when an alarm went off, Sergeant Commando wanted them to sit on the floor, which meant they would have to scramble all over to do so and create confusion. I required them to sit quietly in their seats and not move, which made much more sense. To him this was an offense of his authority. Eventually, common sense ruled, and we did it my way. It pissed him off.

He would hold court in his office like some king. He, not the lieutenant or captain, ruled the yard. The powers that were above him let him rule. They were afraid of him. When he made lieutenant, he was self-righteous, impossible to work with, and constantly nasty to the teachers. He became the senior correctional officer union steward, which I thought was odd, for how could he, being in an argument as a steward, represent rank and file? I always thought this was a conflict of interest. Wardens were afraid of him, and over the years with union support, three of them were transferred.

The final conflict with him was during a staff meeting. I and another teacher would go to their weekly meetings, and he liked to make us look foolish. For example, in our "Bible" there is a section called "The Use of Force." This section was necessary for officers to know when to use force, but was not for teachers. For two weeks prior, he had asked me to define the section. I didn't know, and he tried to make me look bad in a roomful of officers.

"Lockshin, what is the use of force?"

I replied, "Lieutenant Commando, the use of force is when I break a chair over your head for asking me about the use of force!"

The entire room broke up into a fit of laughter. The moral of this is that he never asked me again! When the education department was cut to pieces from 2008 to 2010 due to budget restraints, as a union representative, he could not care less that we went from sixty-two teachers to twelve.

My Classroom

M ost teachers who have a classroom don't like a sterile wall. I was no exception. As a GED teacher and history major, I made sure that the room had lots of math, history, science, and English posters to erase the feeling of four blank walls.

Our education complex consisted of six classrooms, a small office, and a large inmate bathroom. Three of the classrooms and the office had air-conditioning, the rest swamp coolers or fans. I was unlucky to have a classroom with one fan (in my entire career I had an ale unit for two years). For security purposes, the inmate restroom had a glass partition—no enclosed stalls—so when you walked by, you watch inmates poop and pee. This was to make sure no contraband was passed among themselves. Only one inmate from each class could use the restroom at a time. I was the keeper of the piss pass and responsible for writing down when they left and when they came back. I controlled their bodily functions.

The room was very small for the twenty-eight of them, containing chairs and three desks. The swamp cooler never worked in the summer, but worked very well in the winter! At times, the temperature would drop to forty degrees, and we felt we were in a freezer. I can remember one time when it rained and there was a leak in the ceiling; I had a waterfall coming down my front wall. After three hours of heavy downpour, there was three to four inches of water on the floor and the officer still wanted me to run class. I refused because this was a health and safety issue. Our principal agreed with me, so class was canceled.

During the summer months, when it was 100 degrees outside, it was 104 degrees in my room with 100 percent humidity. The swamp cooler didn't work, nor could maintenance ever find the parts to fix it. I had one fan to move hot, humid air. Imagine trying to teach in this environment.

By law, when the temperature reached 102 degrees, we were supposed to send the inmates back to their housing units. This rarely happened. Left to my own devices, I was able to acquire a five-gallon keg and kept it full of ice water.

One problem we had only during the summer was that animals, cats, birds, or gophers would get trapped in the air ducts and the cooler and die there. The stink from their decomposing bodies in that heat was overpowering. One could not run class, and I had to have maintenance clean the ducts once a week during the summer.

Even though we had the inmates for 6.5 hours a day, there were frequent interruptions. We would have alarms go off for various reasons. Inmates would be sent back to their housing units by security. If it started late or the chow hall was short on food, class would start at 8:30 or 9:00 a.m. (the normal starting time was 6:45 a.m.). If the inmate count was off in the buildings, our class would be sent back for count, which made perfect sense for security, but ruined our day.

Motivation and Style

When I first started teaching in the prison system, I was assigned to, as we know, the C yard, which had been named Jurassic Park by those who that it is the most violent yard in the institution, housing inmates that were either there for life or with a sentence nearly as bad.

Although inmates were mandated by the state to obtain their GEDs, I wondered, *Why?* After all, they were not returning to society. The policy is and was that a felon could go to his parole board every few years and have a hearing on his case for the possibility of parole, but this was just pro forma, and the status quo of the industrial would rarely change if they did at all.

The parole board, the felon, and everyone else knew that this was just a dog-and-pony show. For rehabilitation, the board wanted to know a few things.

"Did the felon obtain his GED?"

"What vocational courses did he complete, and was a certification issued?"

"Did he complete the A.A.IN.A classes and sober up?"

"Has he completed or taken any college classes?"

The board and state wanted to know that the felon was trying to make the "time served" worthwhile than just doing nothing.

All the classes, the GED, and certificates were just the "show." The felon, in rare cases, was going nowhere, and time marched on. The truth that custody had no interest to have teachers there at all is a sad enough concept, and we teachers were constantly reminded of their perspective. The consensus was that the inmate was entitled to nothing, and if he was kept in a cell 24-7, that would have been preferred. This show went on and still goes on. So much for redemption and rehabilitation. On the surface, and for public scrutiny, we teachers were told we were doing a great job. In reality, we were totally disliked. The cops, the administration, and we teachers all knew this. In knowing how this system worked, there was a group of teachers who were determined to make the best of a bad situation.

On the E yard, there were many periods of inmate lockdowns—days, weeks, and even months. In our recording system, an "s" time would mean we had no contact or teaching time. For example, if my teaching time was only two days and the rest of the month "s" time due to security lockdowns, the teachers would be blamed for not teaching, even though security had ordered the procedure, so this was the world I taught in.

In public school, if a student was a problem, I wrote demerits, referrals, suspension letters, and called parents. In teaching at the institution, I could not call his mother and say, "Your forty-year-old son didn't do his work." Do you think a grown man who killed his drug partner and doing forty years to life cares about being written up? I doubt it.

So how to motivate them? For the most part, they were society's failures. Sure, they had robbed, stolen, and all the money they had obtained pissed away. I had to find a common ground, which was yes, they had screwed up and been put away, but I wanted them to succeed at something. Education is power, and achieving it step by step would be important to them and myself. I believe now as I did then that even though educationally they were at rock bottom, we could only go up. I told them that on an assignment if four questions were correct over ten, then they got four right and not six wrong, and that next time we would do better.

In working with this clientele, I realized I would have to use skills that worked in the public school and reorganize them here. Not everyone can be a teacher; a person's first words are not "I want to teach." A teacher may know all the bookwork, but when standing in front of a group of students, they fall apart. I was lucky. I had been in sales for thirty years and was comfortable in talking to small or large groups of potential clients. It's called having a command presence, where one feels at ease and making themselves and others interested in the subject at hand. It became easy for me to talk on different topics because I had done so for years.

I can assure you that teaching grown men who have been incarcerated for years is no easy task, especially when many of them who are assigned don't want to be there. These students and I had two classes of twenty-eight. In the beginning, they would be the ones to challenge me. In each class, I had students who had different needs. Some of them had no skills at all. Their brains had been fried due to drug use.

I made mistakes at first. We all do. The student in the classroom sat in racial groups. I started to break this segregation by rearranging the seating to create a more integrated atmosphere. The inmates were so self-segregated on the yard and buildings and had been for many years. I could never change this culture, and I left it alone. I never pushed this issue again.

I explained to my classes that I was here to help them pass the GED and let them know my students would receive a passing grade with any of their assignments. I gave them a sample test, and it was a real eye-opener for them when they failed. I believed that they were better than they thought they were, and with loads of hard work, we began.

I started out at ground zero to find out what they knew and didn't know. With most of these was a ground floor; most were avid readers and rotten in math. Working with fractions was a killer for them. I can remember spending two days with them on division and fractions until they all got the concept. We took very small baby steps in each subject.

One of the objective tests we used was the TABE (Teaching Adult Basic Education), which was given twice a year. This covered comprehension, reading, English, and math. These tests gave us a guideline of where the student was and scores completed. It was hoped that the students' scores improved every six months; if there was no improvement, it underlined where the student needed to improve. However, there was a tiny flaw! Some students would plan to fail or would score in such a way to make it look like they couldn't read or write and had a low IQ. This would keep them in education classes for a much longer time. I had a student whose scores were always low, and one day I asked to borrow a book on chess, which they had no trouble with! I truly had been scammed because he wanted to stay in my class.

My energy was the key to my success. I'd be all over the place; it even looked like I was on roller skates. The effect it had on the inmates was enormous, whose attention was earned by my high-energy teaching. It also helped them to become more interested in the things they were supposed to learn. It didn't matter one bit how I went over material as long as the concept was achieved. I taught by example. I would tell them once they understood the formula of a concept that the light of understanding would go on their faces. They now knew how to do a given problem exercise or written text. My goal for them was to be a winner and a success at something, even if it would mean that they could count two and two and come up with four. I tried never to be stale in presentation of material, nor act like I was bored. I liked to keep myself focused and inspired always looking for new methods of teaching the material to keep the motivation alive. One way of keeping the spark going was to have the class play Jeopardy.

On Fridays I would have two teams of three students compete against each other. The winning team would get two pens and fifty sheets of lined paper per contestant. This went viral with other classes; the inmates wanted their teachers to do this also. I suggest we play one class against another. I was told that (1) it would start a riot and (2) it couldn't be done. My suggestion was to try it and if it didn't work not to do it again. I was given the go-ahead, and it was very successful. We played it every Friday for four years in a row.

Regarding style, you either have it or you don't. I was very lucky that I had been in sales for thirty years and had over the course of that time been able to speak to different groups of people. Having the gift of gab, I was able to do this, but it didn't come easy. Nevertheless, I was able to garner the skills. One of the considerations I had to face was not being a BS artist, as I've said. Felons have a way of seeing right through this, and one's credibility is shot to shit. Inmates can smell when they are being treated in this way.

One of the most important items is to be yourself and to not put on any air. If you're prepared, then it will give the best learning experience for the students involved. Your students look to you to know the material. As a GED teacher, there is an incredible amount of material to present. Many times, I told my students I didn't know the answer to a question but I would find out the answer for them the next day. In teaching adult felons, one has to be at the top of his game or be prepared to be eaten alive.

When I first started, I felt I had twenty-eight pairs of eyes on me all day long, and when we had two three-and-a-half sessions, it was like having fifty-six pairs of eyes. After a while, they stopped watching me and did what they had to do. I always felt relaxed and sat at the tables where they did their assignment. I made it a point to be comfortable with them, and in time, they eased around me. But being aware in my teaching environment was always necessary.

The students and I treated each other with a great deal of respect. When I called on them, it was always Mr. Smith or Mr. Scott. With their permission, I call them by their first names. I never forget that these men were dangerous and could kill me if they so wished. In this way, my goal was that they would find success.

Greeted by the Secret Service

While writing this book, I realized I had to include the incident involving two secret service agents as a threat against the president. You might think the following is untrue; however, I assure you that it is as it happened.

I was working on the D Yard as a GED teacher during President Obama's initial run for election. It was a slow day as the inmates were locked down for some infraction. Three officers and I were discussing the upcoming election when one of them made the comment that he'd like to shoot Obama. Since this was not a bright remark, I will refer to him as Not-SoBright.

He continued with this line of commentary. We told him these comments could be considered as a terrorist threat. These rants continued for days, but other officers did not report this behavior because it would violate their "green machine" brotherhood. After hearing about the different ways Not-So-Bright was going to off our president-to-be, I reported this to our principal.

After reporting what was heard to our principal on a Monday afternoon, on Tuesday morning our warden called, asking to speak to me on the phone.

"Did Officer 'Not-So-Bright' talk about killing the president?"

"How were you made aware of this?"

"Your principal told me. Is it true?"

"I'd rather not say, nor get the officer in trouble."

"If you don't write the information for me, I will make sure that you will come up on charges and lose 10 percent of your pay for twenty-four months."

After deciding that I didn't like Not-So-Bright all that much…
"You'll have my report in an hour."

Once I sent in the report, I thought that was end of that. Boy, was I wrong!

Two weeks later, I was instructed to the warden's office where two secret service agents awaited me. The warden and chief deputy warden advised that these two secret service agents were here to talk to me about Not-So-Bright and his comments. They wanted to interview me about Not-So-Bright's comments since it is their job to investigate any possible threats, real or imagined, regarding the president. They wanted to know how serious Not-So-Bright was.

And so I told them that Mr. No-So-Bright was as dumb as a brick and proceeded to relate another incident that had happened a few years before where Mr. Not-So-Bright had brought in a large snake and threw it on our switchboard operator's desk to create some sensation at work, resulting in a 10 percent fine for two years. When hearing the story of the event, the secret service agents realized that Not-So-Bright was no terrorist threat, but was just a number one schmuck.

Needless to say, our genius was fined another 10 percent for twenty-four months and assigned to the mail room for ten months, the place people were placed when they fucked up. Not-SoBright was with other screwups like himself.

When leaving work one day, he told me that I had fucked him. My reply was, "You fucked yourself. Own it. It's all yours!" People always want to blame others and never want to take ownership of their own screwups.

The Fourth Estate and Mr. TV

D uring my tenure at Lancaster Prison, I was asked to develop a newsletter for the education department. My buddy Tom helped me on this project (I would be Perry White and Clark Kent, and he would be my faithful Lois Lane. The reader will find a copy of our paper at the end of this book).

The prison had a monthly publication devoted to stories about correction officers and everyone else, but nothing on the education department or of any importance to our department. Tom, I, and Miguel (our principal) came to the conclusion that we should have an outlet for what was going on in our department, tooting our own horn, so to speak. This would give us a forum and provide a basis for what we were doing, such as GED and TABE testing. We concluded that the paper would come out once a month. Tom and I would be the reporters, write the editorials, print the material, and distribute it to the teachers. We would publish what was important to us and our department.

We were given carte blanche to cover anything. The paper was worked on during our prep period, which was the last period of the day, or when the yard was locked down, which was quite often. One good thing that came out of this was that all the "Yentas" (buys bodies) and rumor mongers were able to see their rumors in print. The paper ran from 2000 to 2003 and was quite successful. We then decided that if the written word was successful, why not use prison institutional TV system and put canned classroom material on during the year instead of meaningless programs the inmates were watching? Tom had been a part-time cameraman for the movie industry. He had a great deal of knowledge setting up a video shot, and we both wrote material for shooting classroom videos. Students participated in the taping, which brought them to work together. Topics ranged from basic math to essay writing. This allowed those inmates who were not in class, who had regular day jobs, to partake in watching these programs on their time off. This program worked well because it gave another two to three hundred inmates the opportunity to prepare for their GED without being in the classroom (our use of videotaping was done by the seat of our pants; we navigated this virgin territory with no set guidelines).

Sacramento had developed its own system for providing canned programming, ending our efforts after a year. These two programs provided us with a great deal of satisfaction, as it created other methods for the department to be successful.

Teaching is a difficult position, be it in public school or a state-run institution. It's doubly hard when the inmates assigned to school or who want his GED were incarcerated forever or who had extensive use of drugs. They were difficult to teach, but there were there and we taught them.

Imagine working with adult males who had been out of school for twenty or thirty years who might have been thrown out of school after the seventh or eighth grade. The simplest math problem was difficult. The question and answer had to be simple, in a language they understood. So I invented prison math. Some examples include the following:

Example 1
(Every inmate knew the answer to this one.)
Q. How many grams in an ounce?
A. "28, if you're cutting up coke."

Example 2
Q. "If the prison yard has a quarter-mile track and you walk it two to three times a week, how many miles will you have walked in thirty years?"

Example 3

Q. If you receive $200 in June from Aunt Flo and you want to spend money at the canteen, how much can you spend when the state keeps 55 percent of what you get?

Example 4

Q. You make a gallon of pruno (illegal alcohol), give away one pint to Sam and one quart to Fred. How much do you have left to get stinking drunk?

Example 5

Q. In a pinochle tournament, you and your partner win 30 percent of sixty games. What is the number of games won?

Example 6

Q. You get a 16 oz can of coffee in a package. One quarter you give to Sam, 3/8ths you gibe to Nick. What's left for you?

Example 7

Q. You earn $0.18 per hour. After twenty-eight days, you made $19.00. How much is left after 55 percent is taken out for restitution?

Example 8

Q. Sam and Nick go to the movies and spend $38 for tickets. You go to the movies and pay $20. What is your change?

Teaching math this way was very helpful and allowed the inmates to grasp math concepts. They learned, and I learned a new method. We all improved!

The Inmate

E very inmate I ever had to deal with would always say "I'm innocent!" or "The state fucked me!" and of course I always agreed with them. The prison has 4,400 "guests of the state" who are not guilty. Of course, if you were to see an inmate's C file, which can weigh six to twenty pounds, "Mr. Innocent" has been placed away from society for twenty-five years to life without parole simply because he was caught.

Let me give you two examples. The first "Mr. Right" felt he got fifteen years to life on a bum rap. A second striker. He ran a DUI stop because the car he was driving was stolen, had five ounces of blow under the front seat, and was carrying a .50 caliber pistol. He was, therefore, totally surprised he "struck out" on his third strike.

My second example is "Joe," who was the choir director on the A Yard, the "Honor Yard," where inmates went to if they were discipline-free for five years. Joe had been a piano player in bars and had convinced himself and others that he had been in the military. Nothing was further from the truth. He was a lounge lizard who was doing twenty years for being a flasher and assaulting little boys.

I will say that inmates, until they feel that they can trust you, will try and BS you. As an ex-Brooklyn lad where everyone BS's everyone else, I never bought into their "snow jobs."

Once this objective of trust was established, inmates and I had a bond of trust. Never lie to them. Always be honest and straight up. Be firm, fair, and treat them like people. If asked, they would, on a one-on-one basis, say what they were in for. This could have been checked from their file, but whatever they did throughout their lives was of little interest to me in the here and now.

It's amazing how they could adjust to the same routine day in and day out. Every Monday they would have oatmeal for breakfast. This never deviated. It would be expected as long as they are in prison, which, for many, was a lifetime of Monday oatmeal. If there were a good part for oatmeal, at least they knew it was Monday.

Their cell house was approximately ten feet wide and eleven feet long. Originally, each cell was to house one prisoner, but each housed two prisoners. With two bunk beds, leaving about six cubic feet for each inmate, a sink and toilet, the area became pretty crowded, leaving only a four-foot gap between the bed and sink. No room to turn around. You might get lucky and have a 360-pound cellmate named Tiny who would of course have the top bunk. If the two of you were unlucky to be "locked down" for a day, week, or month (or longer), you would be cell fed all three meals. Just you and Tiny. Usually when meals came and went, one of you would be taking a crap. As for cleanliness, you washed out of the sink. And if the conditions remained the same—if the guards were not pissed off—you got a shower every fourth day. Maybe.

Normally, the housing units were spotlessly clean, but during lockdowns, they stank. When entering such a unit after a week of lockdown, the building stank of unwashed bodies. A stink that hung in the air like a cloud. Normally the inmates with exception are very hygienic in their appearance: clothing neat and cells perfectly clean. Most cells were so clean one could eat off the floor.

The cost for providing three meals a day (two hot, one cold) is about $2.65 per day. Mostly all starch and carbs of nearly insufficient quantities; they are always hungry. They are each allowed a hot plate and make the most of cooking Top Roman, and a host of other ingredients. They are allowed to spend a maximum of $150 per month from the canteen. They are allowed a forty-pound package every quarter, and the material in these packages must be in a clear container from a specific vendor.

Every item has a dollar value: soups, coffee, sardines, cookies—anything. The concrete tables on the yard are the gambling casinos—

poker, craps, and twenty-one. It's amazing to watch the inmates at play. Oh, and by the way, if your debt is not paid in one month, you're beaten up. The second month you don't pay it, you're dead.

Life hangs by a curious thread at the prison. All inmates are very polite, never to "disrespect" a fellow inmate, because that could be fatal to the insulter. There are times when things are funny. An inmate who had less than five months to parole was going to be married upon release. He had written her that he had worked on a crab ship for the last six months in Alaska; like the most dangerous catch, no one could have gotten in contact with him. He asked me if I could bring in a tape measure.

"The tape measure would provide for my suit," they said.

I replied, "I'm not your tailor. Get measured when you get out."

Inmates have asked me the oddest things. For example, I had a student with one tooth in his mouth. It looked like a fang. He had a problem with this tooth and wondered if he needed a root canal from the dentist. I suggested he have it pulled and get a mouthful of dentures.

Inmates are Bible scholars. They can quote passages from the Bible twenty-four hours a day. One would think you're at the Vatican in Rome. With all the time on their hands they are avid readers and great soap opera TV fans. I often would wonder if these men, if paroled, would hit the bars or church first.

I would ask those who had life without parole, "Why not just end it? Why put up with fifty or more years of the same dull routine?" After all, they'd save the state (you and I) a ton of money. The idea of killing themselves was horrible… but to kill others was OK.

An Overview

L et's get real here. If not for the money, then what was the reason? I believed I could help inmates and enable them to have
an opportunity for success. After all, those incarcerated are the failures of society. I chose to work in a sub-culture of what some feel is
the "refuse of humanity." I am no Mother Teresa. My objective was
always to provide a useful education and the proper tools so that
upon parole, if ever, the inmate might become an effective member
of society. One should understand that in the days of old, it was
common to either execute prisoners or place them where they were
neither seen nor heard. The English realized that by transporting
inmates to faraway places like Botany Bay and New South Wales
they achieved their purpose.

These people were far enough away that they could do English
society little or no harm. Additionally, their children might become
worthwhile citizens to the crown. The Spanish and French put
inmates to work during the same period. The theft of a loaf of bread,
such as Jean Val Jean in Victor Hugo's *Les Misérables*, could get one
to twenty years on a galley. Some people would like to have the moon
or small planet as a prison colony whereby the inmates could gov-
ern themselves. I once asked my class of students where they would
be safer living, on Catalina Island as a colony or the prison? The
answer, surprisingly enough, was that they would feel safer in prison.
I thought they would believe that a *Lord of the Flies* system could
work for them.

This position as an educator is not for the weak of spirit. It takes
about five to six months before one is granted a position. The process

includes a background check that goes back to the womb. There is the psychological exam to make sure one is of a sound mind. The final step is a two-part interview process. Upon successfully completing these tasks, one becomes a "correctional educator." There is a forty-hour training session at the given institution that covers all the do's and don'ts. Following the training session, one is assigned to a yard or facility where often a supervisor falsely places you like a square peg in a round hole. Everyone else is placed the same way—from the teaching staff, the inmates, and supervisors. I can honestly say that when I finally saw the classroom where I could be teaching, my first thought was, "What the hell am I doing here?" I soon learned that my fellow colleagues had the same thought.

The prison is and was a maximum security facility. I was assigned to the C Yard, which had the sobriquet of "Jurassic Park." Every day was considered a holiday no different from the Fourth of July or Halloween. You never knew what waiting around the comer. This translates into daily stabbings, fistfights between ethnic groups, and the sound of correctional officers in the towers (known as gunners) firing warning shots when things got bad. Then there were the lockdown days, weekly or monthly, when the inmates were confined in their housing units for twenty-four hours a day. This was the new world I was entering as a teacher.

The first class I taught was called adult basic education 2/3. Essentially, this meant that there would be a mixed class ranging from fourth through eighth grade. It consisted of fifteen Blacks, twelve Mexicans, and two White students. About ninety-five people of these students were "lifers." This meant they were never going to be paroled back into society. Their sentences ranged from twenty-five years to life, or life without the possibility of parole (nicknamed L-wop for short). The students had a question for me on the first day: "Why should they learn?" My answer: "Your bodies may rot, but don't let your brain rot. Knowledge is power." This was especially true if a student wanted to achieve his GED and succeed at something.

As a teacher with the incarcerated, I only have a six-and-a-half-hour day to make changes in their lives. It is similar to a lion tamer in a cage with hungry lions, except that as a teacher I had no whip.

All I had was a compendium of knowledge to share and my communication skills. The reader must realize that, as a teacher, I was a guest in their environment. The goal was the leave alive and well at the end of the day. The students were in my world during the school days and therefore had to obey certain rules of civility and behavior. The classrooms, visiting areas, and the chapels are neutral zones where violence is not condoned by the inmates. I also understood the rules that the inmates have in their world. The unwritten rule of respect has to be followed. The constant racial and sexual tension among the inmates oozed out of every pore in the institution.

As a teacher in this setting, I am alone. I have an alarm that I wear, and the correctional officers are everywhere, but if the students wish to kill or harm me, they can do so with ease.

They know it and let you know it as well. I teach with a methodology of respect. I respect them, and this is reciprocated. I am not the enemy, and the guards and the systems are otherwise known as such. Is there brutality in this system? Yes, there is. I have seen inmates stabbed and observed riots, but never in the classroom. Was I afraid of these students? No. I am aware of them, but not afraid of them. I am comfortable sitting at their desk working on assignments with them, but I am always aware of my surroundings. It's like having a new eye in the back of your head and ears like an antenna My level of comfort puts the students at ease. Most of all, I treat them like human beings.

I can honestly say that after seventeen years of teaching in this system, it was still a lot of fun and was enjoyable. The work was challenging and interesting. As in any organization, I find that management can be the bone of contention. Managers can be dishonest and forget that they were once teachers who have graduated to a management position. This is not just sour grapes. I achieved my master's of arts degree in educational administration in January 2006. I found colleagues in the same classes who, when they became administrators, had forgotten all the information they had diligently studied but never used. At the Lancaster State Prison, we have a terrific principal, vice principal, and like regular public schools, some others are good at their jobs and some are mediocre. However, the principal, as the captain of a ship, must set the tone for all the teachers and administrators.

The principal promotes the success or failure of all teachers by promoting the development of stewardship. The steward in an organization is responsible for preparing its mission statement or the vision of a better organization. The steward is not only a leader but also included in the flow of the organization. As a teacher, part of this culture is that the students do well on their school work, their GED exams, and graduate because of it. By culture, I mean that we support the goals of education at New Horizons Adult School. This is the name we have given the school so that it is presentable to society, and that we are proud of it; ergo, not just an entity in a prison facility. The teacher must accept the students for who they are. The mission statement should be concise, to the point, and most of all, simple to learn. The purpose of the school is to make a contribution to the education of the students in the prison. In institutional management, the vice principal must be willing to listen to teachers and hear what they are saying without judgment. Often they have a belief that there is a hidden agenda, that a teacher is out to get them. Just because a teacher disagrees with a manager does not mean they are defiant, but rather they have an opinion of their own, which may not deal with the issues at that particular moment.

As in any organization, there is the problem of conflict resolution. Principals and their managers are not very good at reducing tensions and disagreements by producing a quick fix. Many of us have left meetings with issues that are unaddressed. Most of us are passionate about our job, the students we serve, and the curriculum we teach. Such passions will evaporate when we don't have the opportunity to communicate with management or others. The usual assumption is that an issue will just disappear and go away, but this leaves us frustrated. The pressure can build up, unite the tensions and frustrations as they come to a head and a situation erupts. Anything may trigger an explosion. We teachers hope that managers will deal with difficult situations and work with conflict resolution, but we have come to the conclusion that this is a pipe dream. Most managers are more worried about their egos than getting things done. Some live in a world of their own kingdom, with each kingdom having its own rules and policies.

An example of this can be seen in the way the prison is divided: yards A–D and minimum. The first four are maximum security, and each yard has a captain who oversees the policies and procedures that are mandated by the Department of Corrections. One would make the assumption the policies are followed to the letter, but this is not the case. Each captain manages the yard to his/her own standards, even though specific rules are in place, vis-à-vis procedures that occur on the A Yard may not be the same with those in the D Yard. This creates confusion because written policy is sometimes overlooked. So what happens is that there is both a written and unwritten policy.

One of the greatest issues I faced as a teacher was the lack of communication in the institution that I worked. More than likely, this issue challenges everyone who works here. Most of the time when working outside of teaching I would feel like a mushroom, placed in a closet and fertilized. This is a common issue we all face. Information is seldom passed down to the teacher in a timely manner and is watered down or full of misinformation, which makes it hard to decipher. On top of this, rumors abound and many half-truths spread within the walls of this facility. For example, like in public school, we have to achieve a superior grade to be accredited; otherwise, we can lose it. Whenever the accreditation team comes to this prison, we receive poor grades for communication skills. This team gives the teaching staff high marks in carrying out its mission. Sometimes, however, management passes their failure on to us, and we receive a poor evaluation. We have submitted proposals to management on how to create better communication within the department and facility. This has often fallen on deaf ears. The educating staff has been made the scapegoat for the lack of the school's progress. This has been a continuous issue for many years. The teachers have used this motto regarding communication: "If it's not in writing, it didn't happen."

As teachers, we always hope that leadership will provide a potential for learning throughout the institution. Supervision must have a vision for the mission of the school. Leadership can work with individual personalities and make sure that we teachers and students have the recourses we need. This is a communal goal and why we are here. Managers must possess the following: be a good listener, have situational awareness, be able to grow, and most of all, be the keystones in the building process of the educational community. Strong leadership should want the staff to provide input and ask such questions as the following:

- Does the staff have an awareness of what is going on?
- Do people feel a strong sense of loyalty?
- Do the teachers believe that management has an interest in them?

The educational leaders must provide direction: good, bad, or indifferent. But they must do the best job possible and have honesty, integrity, and most of all, ethics. The concept of building a community and commitment within this facility is different at best, and without it, there can only be chaos.

As teachers, we are committed to provide quality education to our students, but this is not the only obligation. Teachers and management need to meet on a regular basis to discuss security and educational business. There can be a negative side to this when teachers are denied a serious involvement in decision making. We cannot be fully effective with our peers, students, or anyone else without having the opportunity for redress. As a teacher, I have little time during the school day to deal with sundry matters. It is a given that teachers and managers in the school systems are overworked and there is never enough time. The New Horizon Adult School is no different. Why would teachers want to take on any additional responsibility? There is a faculty advisory committee made up of teachers to discuss and work on issues that affect the entire school. The committee discusses problems with the warden. The minutes of all committee meetings are sent to teachers so that they may have clarification on any issue. The committee was established to address policies and procedures from the Department of Corrections to bring about changes to the prison on educational or security matters. Prior to implementing this committee, there was continuous friction between the managers and teachers.

Teachers and managers should do the following:

- Make good use of time management
- Provide positive examples
- Make contact with others' schools that succeed academically so they can see for themselves possible successful methods

Some of those may include the following:

- Trust and confidence among all teach members
- Involvement in decision making
- Honest and open communication for all members
- High expectations
- Supportive staff members
- Be caring and have the ability to share
- Have a sense of humor
- School rituals, such as GED graduations
- GED testing on a regular basis

The above notwithstanding, there are those at the prison who are never happy or satisfied and prefer the negative approach. They

- view students as a problem rather than an opportunity;
- don't search for new ideas;
- complain, criticize, and distrust new ideas, approaches, or suggestions;
- rarely share ideas, materials, and have no solutions or input on any issue;
- exhibit motivational apathy and loss of creativity; and
- express fatalism about one's work.

All the issues that the regular teacher has to deal with, we also face. As in any organization, the few have to carry the load of the many. Teachers suffer from four major areas. Whether in public school settings or in prison, they are the same. These four are (1) burnout, (2) fatalism about work, (3) preoccupation with comfort zone, and (4) resistance to change. Let's examine each one:

Burnout

Burnout is a syndrome that everyone faces regardless of their job. Most teachers face this about the tenth or eleventh year. The job itself is not tiring. It's that the expectations have changed. As teachers, most of us enjoy the activity that we are paid for; however, we have to deal with supervisors and managers who are far from the classroom and the stressors we face. Let's be honest. Most of us would agree that those who move up to management could not teach anyway, nor would they be as successful as we were. They are to serve the school/prison administrators, and they look at numbers and the end result. There is nothing in error in looking at the end result, as long as the end does not justify the means. Burnout comes when management does not listen to the people who know how the system worked. This is not true in every case, but true enough for most. The teachers get tired and so bone-weary that no one seems to hear them, and what happens then can be fatal to that teacher, which leads to number two: fatalism about one's work.

Fatalism

By fatalism, I mean a slow death of the teacher's awareness to do the best job they can do. The approach becomes that whatever is done is never enough or has no significance to the outcome or the project; missing school is no longer important. The professional is just surviving another day/week/month until they retire. Any ideas that are developed for the benefit of the school or inmate student are usually shot down only for the purpose of not causing unwanted change. Some teachers who have this methodology tell teachers not to bring up any ideas that are out of the ordinary because it will be one more thing they don't want to do and to just go through the motions. Many people do because it is out of the comfort zone. They are happy with the status quo and don't want to rock the boat, are happy with apathy, and don't want to see any changes on the horizon. If things worked well in the present, they will fight like the devil to make sure that new changes will never be made. Sometimes a good or great idea will be presented but will die an ugly death if that idea is not presented by the teachers.

Preoccupation with Comfort Zone

The Department of Rehabilitation and Correction will soon have over two hundred thousand inmates in the system. The Lancaster State Prison, where I worked, was built to house about two thousand. Currently, there are over 4,500 inmates and are heavily overcrowded. The state wanted to have special state bonds that the voters will pass to increase the number of prisoners in California, a fool's parade unless something is done now or in the very near future. Otherwise, the system will collapse. Taxpayers are tired of paying $27,000 per year so that inmates can sit on their asses, eat two meals a day, watch soap operas, and sue on frivolous matters. The State of California plays the old shell game where the player moves the bean and one pays to find it. Here, the Dept. of Corrections plays the same game, sans the beam.

We have a system that we call the Department of Rehabilitation and Corrections, and IO has always felt that this name was an oxymoron. We don't rehabilitate, nor do we correct. We just warehouse people for a number of years. The dates of the release and the myth of trying to educate are not important. The teachers do the best job they can (for the most part) but are two prong attacks, the first of which is the inmates who just want to do their time. Maybe they want an education; maybe they don't. The time fills six and a half hours a day, and if the teacher is lucky, something will click and the inmate may become motivated. The second attack is the system itself, and most usually, the corrections officers provide the security of the institution. They are there for a day's wage. They could not care about the inmates and consider them to be the dregs of humanity, yet provide the officers with their overtime, which can provide an income of over $100,000 per year, a nice amount of money for just having a GED or high school diploma. The correction officers, just like the inmates, I could care less if the inmates are educated as long as the prison rules are carried out to the letter and are obeyed. Ergo, the teacher is caught between two parallel universes at each end of the spectrum, and both have the same common grounds. The correctional system couldn't care less if the inmate receives an education or not. They, the inmates, are there to serve time.

Resistance to Change

W hen people ask me if prison really is like the defunct TV series "Oz," I have to laugh before I answer because Hollywood created a series for the media that had very little reality in it when compared to the real world. Do inmates make weapons, have fights, and have sex riots? Of course they do, but that is not the total reality. Time, for the inmate, seems never to end and drags very slowly, the monotony of their routine ever present. Time has no meaning, but nor does it stand still. I have asked inmates who walk the yard, "How many miles will you have walked around the quarter-mile track in twenty-five years?" So far, no one has provided me with an answer. Even though the state provides for all their needs, I have noticed that inmates seem to deteriorate. By this, I mean that over the years, inmates lose teeth, hearing, body texture, and of course, suffer from an improper diet. The prison fare is no bargain, and the state spends about $2.50 per day on cheap staples.

The teachers must understand how the inmate culture works. One could say "It's us versus them," but it's more than that. The prison culture is made of many ethnic groups. The majority groups are (1) African American, (2) Hispanic, and (3) White. These three groups are the power center of the inmate population. For example, each group has its own area of influence, such as the mess hall, day-rooms, the housing, and exercise yard. For one group to impose itself on another group's territory is considered disrespectful and can lead to violence. When there is an ethnic class, it is usually over territory. In the summer, for instance, Hispanics will shave their heads as a sign of solidarity. In addition, one racial group will not enter another's territory without the permission of the leaders called the shot callers. In the system that I have worked, the predominant sex is male. For the male gender, the best way to achieve maturity is to have a successful male role model, someone a child can look up to. In the harsh socio-economic conditions of African and Hispanic culture, there normally is no positive role model, but rather one based on criminal behavior (gangs, drugs, etc.). One finds a home environment consisting of one or no parent at home to provide for these individuals a caring, sharing family atmosphere. Rather, the father, mother, sibling, and/or other family dynamic are recreated here behind bars. Most, but not all, of the inmates in the Lancaster State Prison originate from the generally poor or economically disadvantaged backgrounds. This is true in the public system. Boys appear to have a dominant nature compared to girls and dominate classroom activities due to the perpetuation of gendered roles in society. Male students enjoy classroom participation but do poorly in reading and writing. The conclusion is that boys are most likely to be underachievers, whereas girls are overachievers when it comes to behavior in the school setting.

Most of the men in prison started out as boys having problems in the neighborhood and the school. Poor behavior gores them into trouble. The inability to function in society where they were in the lower strata of the economic scale meant that school success was not as important as local culture. How to survive was paramount. The gang was the family they never had, and the ability to earn easy cash from selling drugs or contraband was all that mattered. There is another point that needs to be covered here in this socioeconomic culture that plagues the prison system, and two sources that provide information on these minority groups that have increased the prison population. First, Davis (1995) wrote that the sale of drugs has provided for longer prison terms for Blacks and Hispanics. He provides the following demographic: 3 percent of white men, 23 percent of Hispanic men, and 20 percent of Black men between 1965 and1969 have served time in prison by their early thirties. The second source, Vincent Schrader (2004), writes that African Americans have a twelve times greater risk and Hispanic Americans a nine times greater risk than those of a White ethnic group being incarcerated.

Drug sentencing has increased dramatically over the last ten to twenty years. It is the way to make the quick dollar when there is no other way to move up the social ladder. Charles Kawasaki (2002) wrote that from 1981 to 2020, California prisons had had a 25 percent increase in drug offenders. This impacts the poorer inner city communities, again mainly young Black and Hispanic males. Young people, especially, are being incarcerated for drugs in these communities where the school dropout rate is high and the emolument outlook bleak. The sale of drugs becomes the economic basis for the community. Drugs provide easy money for the gangs or dealers on the street comer. The individual will be sent to an institution where he will be welcome with open arms by members of the family or gang already incarcerated there.

The California prison system is overcrowded and ill-managed, containing places of violence, physical abuse, and hate, thus making them breeding grounds that perpetuate and magnify the same type of behavior over and over again. America has the highest number of people incarcerated in the world. We now house 25 percent of the world-reported prisoners. According to FBI documentation, we imprison 756 inmates per one hundred thousand persons. Included in this are about five million people who left prison and under probation or parole supervision. About one out of thirty-one adults in this country is in prison, jail, or on parole. This is a very high financial amount for the taxpayers to sustain.

I can remember when I started with the department in May that most of the inmates I worked with had very long terms or life without the possibility of parole. They were convicts, a breed unto themselves. They self-governed each group's behavior, and if there were incidents such as lockdowns or riots, these issues were handled quickly. Everyone understood their standing in the convict' institution. Things have changed within the last few years. More and more inmates who have come from the county jails are incarcerated for drug and/or mental illness, most for nonviolent crimes. Drug offenders are returning to prison like a revolving door. Most of the inmates who return are usually associated with a gang—both from the streets and in prison. They monitor the use of illegal drugs in the neighborhoods from whence they came, and in the prisons as well. We are dealing with inmates who have a network throughout all thirty-three prisons.

One might ask, "What is the behavior of the group of people that you are teaching?" The answer is that inmate behavior is like no other. One must think of predatory animal—in this case, a thinking animal (but the use of thought could be debated elsewhere). This animal is always watching and observing what the correctional officer, free staff, and teachers are doing twenty-four hours a day. Remember, the inmate has plenty of time to watch and observe. Any and all information is collected and stored by inmate's leaders so it can be retrieved at a later date. The inmates watch and watch, seeking out any movement or piece of information that can be used to their advantage.

As a member of CDC, one might think that time passes slowly for the inmate. It can, especially when the yard is locked down and there is no inmate movement. Yet the inmate rationale is to get whatever they can from anybody at the least cost to themselves. By "least cost," I mean assaulted by fellow inmates or just stealing things that they can barter or sell to others. If a profit can be gained, then the inmate will attempt it. But suppose the inmate gets caught. Well, that is the risk they take. The inmate will be disciplined and might be sent to "Ad Seg," otherwise known as "the hole." In Ad Seg, the inmate is locked up for twenty-three hours out of every twenty-four hours and, for the last hour, can use a small exercise yard. Consider this exercise yard the same size when you go to the animal shelter. He will stay in this area until sentence is carried out and then returned to his cell block on the yard. This downtime is considered "bad time" and has to be made up for time lost. Sometimes this time is added to his sentence. The rule of thumb is that the inmate knows how the system and game works. Sometimes he wins, and sometimes he loses.

This world that I've worked in is a highly dangerous place. Consider it as a place where 90 percent of the time things and the yards run smoothly. But it's that ten persons that can be a killer. One must always have attention to the surroundings and develop a sixth sense as a way of protection. It's always the right thing to do. This does not mean that one has to be in a constant state of frenzy waiting for something to happen, but it does create a high level of awareness for the surroundings around them. Even though I am relaxed in a classroom of twenty-nine inmates, I am aware of where I am and make sure that I have my whistle and alarm at all times. This is a good time to mention how management works in the system.

Teacher management works the same way in a Gilbert and Sullivan operetta, *H.M.S. Pinafore*, especially the captain's refrain of "handling only a partnership." Managers have a certain style that holds them in good stead among themselves: que será. Don't get me wrong. There are some very good and outstanding managers that I have known who did their job, never pushed the job onto someone else, never passed the buck, nor went over to the dark side. They are the managers who have shown their personal best and lead by example. Then we have all the rest: the 90 percent who are dullards and slackers, the paper pushers, finger pointers, and twofaced backstabbers. I think that covers most of them. Oh wait—there are also the managers, the ones who will boggle you with BS, but when it comes down to getting the job done, they are elsewhere, pointing to the failures of others for the most part, or are apathetic or clueless. Sad to say the fault is not their own. They have been led down the garden path of mediocrity. These bunglers and plodders resent those of us who will get the job of education done and do it well. In this case scenario, one would believe that a manager, any manager with half a brain, will be pleased that a job or task is successfully completed and, once again, they are made to look good. This may or may not happen because in the manager's zeal, they may change the teacher's yearly evaluation for doing too good a job. We have had principals who give great talks, and what is amazing to me is that the assistant principals will nod their head, agree with whatever comes out of the principal's head, but have no clue as to what he had said when asked.

I previously mentioned the "dark side." Let me explain. With all jobs, there is always the teaching that one can climb the corporate ladder and rise up from the primeval ooze of mediocrity, but with teaching in the CDC, that ooze becomes a stink that does not wear off. Teachers can become vice principals in one or two ways. The first is to put in an application to be placed on the list for management testing. Once the test is passed, the individual can interview at any one of the thirty-three prison locations. Consider this fact that the people who are going to interview you can't really be bothered, but do it anyway to break up their day. They already know who will get the job from the "ole boys" club. The rule is that managers will confer amongst themselves and pick out someone like themselves for the vice principal position offered.

The second method in picking for vice principal is through the vice principal acting post, which is supposed to be a temporary acting position. At our institution, the choice was done in a fair and equitable manner. Consider the fact that there were two teachers who had all the qualifications for the acting role and one teacher who had brownnosed all the managers. You can guess who was given the position (one must remember that as soon as the teacher was elevated to the vice principal position, any element of being a classroom teacher was washed away by the "dark side"). I call this the "dark side" because any teacher who moves up the chain has a habit of forgetting what it was like to be in the classroom and having to deal with morons in management who bothered you with mindless pap while you were trying to teach. They have morphed into management with the impression that they have always been a manager whether or not they knew anything about the job. Any resemblance of teaching was washed away by the mantel of "vice principal." It was like amnesia. You forgot that you came from the ranks. These managers forget that, as a teacher, there is a union contracted to follow, and even though they agreed with this as a teacher, it's forgotten as a vice principal. As a vice principal, what do you are about union grievances? The principal gives these people the right to manage their realm as they see fit. The words that was fought for as a teacher—the ethics and team members—likely become akin to a deadly anathema when that person becomes manager.

For example, teachers have to sign in by six twenty and at their work stations by six thirty. When they leave at the end of the day, they must sign out by two fifteen. However, if they arrive late, leave early, or don't sign out, they may be written up by their direct supervisor. They couldn't care less what happens during the day, as long as people sign in and out when they are supposed to. Any work that happens during that time is a bonus.

Reality

Although I may have sounded bitter about my entire teaching experience at this institution, this is not exactly true. I have loved teaching in the classroom here from the beginning. I took to this job like a duck to water, and in May 2012, put in my retirement papers. I elected to do this while I still had brain cells left, because working for the Department of Corrections has been one whacked-out roller-coaster ride, a real E ticket. If I told people what really goes on here, they wouldn't believe me and think I had made it up; however, any member of this system would swear on a stack of bibles that nothing was made up. I can honestly say that I have never punched anyone out that I worked with, but there have been times that were sorely tested. In this system of working for the State of California and the prison system, I have never observed so many people working so hard to avoid work. At the beginning of my journey in May 1996, I asked myself, "Wow, what did I get myself into?" I was determined to keep my sanity even if others did not think I would. I had always told myself that when being at the prison was no longer any fun I'd retire and find other employment. There have been many times that I almost threw in the towel, but I told myself, "Just one more time."

One of the key major gripes of mine (only one?) is that the system wastes a lot of time, money, energy, talent, and people. We the teachers who do the job assigned us try to instill the point of education not only to the inmates but also to the correction officers. With one group (inmates), this has a positive effect; with the other group (the officers), what we do is a waste of time. It has proven that education/vocation programs do reduce recidivism. We who have been here a while realize that minority groups such as African and Hispanic Americans have increased dramatically, possibly due to socioeconomic means. Who pays for this? The fact of the matter is, we all do; the budget in 1977 was about $3.8 billion where it was $6.5 billion in 2011. Governor Brown somehow thinks it wise to send approximately 19,000 inmates back to the countries they came from, placing them in local jails. It is a great magic act.

We pay more for incarceration in this state than any other. To house an inmate in CDCR, it costs about $55,000 per year, most of the costs being eaten up by payroll (after all, to feed the inmate only costs about $2.60 per day). In other states, their systems pay much less and have smoother running programs for the staff and the inmates. For inmates on death row in California, this costs an extra $10,000 a year, where such inmates only due from old age, indigestion, and boredom.

The close association between illiteracy and crime is important, because for many inmates, had they succeeded in school, they might never have dropped out or wound up at prison. Sure, the drug explosion made people who would be nonfunctioning in the hood have the ability to make a lot of money by dealing drugs, prostitution, or anything else. They could make $500 a day just by standing on the comer and paying a little protection for untaxed money. Who would not do it? Of course, their life may end suddenly, but that is the chance they take. I know inmates who tell me they would never come back to prison if they were released today. We know this statement is all BS, because if let out today, they would be back in one day or many as long as ninety days. They are creatures of habit. I know of many inmates who had good-paying jobs on the streets but were drawn to the concept of fast money like a magnet; it was always too good to tum down until they got caught and came back to prison. A student told me how the system screwed him. It went like this: his claim to fame was breaking into homes, and he never would be caught until he was! He said the deal was if he admitted to the break-ins, he would get six years and only do half of the sentence. He felt that he was being set up by the state, turned the deal down, and wound up serving fifteen years instead of six.

"The state fucked me," he said.

"You fucked yourself," I told him.

I believed in what I did at the prison. Again, it was not for the money (although that paid well). All of us who do teach use any methodology to get the job done—stimulation, motivational material on the walls in the classroom, even a little Christmas tree in my room for the holidays. There is a bookcase in my room filled with paperback books, which can be loaned out for a oneweek period.

None of my books have ever been stolen, by the way, and it is used on the honor system. I try to encourage the same high expectations from the inmates, such as

1. Activities that engage students in the learning process
2. Use everyday issues for social/life skills
3. Incorporate learning by
   a. Small groups
   b. Accountability
4. Student-teacher interaction
5. Prompting the students to explain (I want to know how they got the answer)
6. The use of effective strategies
7. Modern technology
   a. Closed-circuit TV
   b. Multimedia instruction
8. Developed self-awareness
9. Get rid of the tail-wagging syndrome: "I am a failure, and I will fail."

The bottom line is we, as teachers, are here to provide a service, and we should do that service. We must use all the tools that are at our disposal.

Motivating the inmate is extremely important; one cannot motivate people any more than empower them. The main ingredient for me is that I and my students both have to be contagious. I do not care what mood I am in. Once I am though the gates coming to work, all my shitty attitudes are forgotten while I am there. No one wants to see a sour face, especially here; where sour is the most de la jou. I try to drop my problems and bring a happy mood because that is contagious, and the students pick up my energy. I would fly around the room, and they would ask how much coffee I had. Truly, education and the tools therein have always proved that there is light at the end of the tunnel. Sure, inmates will get their GEDs, take correspondence courses for whatever degree they seek out. Unfortunately, despite our impact, there is not much of a fund for teachers.

The California Department of Corrections and Recidivism makes me cringe. "Corrections" and "recidivism" are some of my most-hated key words. What do we "correct," and what lends toward "recidivism"? As it appears, these two words make up for buzzwords for the entire system. Everyone yeses them, and no one is sure what they really mean. While many believe these two constructs are a load of crap, there are some people out there who believe this wholeheartedly, that working with these words in mind will act like some sort of cure for cancer. Fixing a system is difficult work and nearly always requires several things in order to do so.

The Bed and Board Modality

Once the prisoner has reached his "final destination" in the state prison, the cost of room and board should be on him and/or their family. Let us assume that we pay the inmate for the work that he does in the vocational shop. Half of a month's wage would pay for their room and board; one quarter would be placed in a trust account to be used when he is paroled (in this way, the institution will have more than the $200 in gate money when he leaves).

Money Makes the World Go Round

C ut out all the overtime. People will have to work straight shifts. The state complains about all this money going out the door. Officers, dentists, and nurses who are making $1,000 in overtime only state that they are living here, have no life except for the extra time. The overtime becomes a "cash cow" for anyone who is allowed to work it. People will say, "But there are times we need it." Okay, for those times, have it. There is considerable waste of state money and only one way to fix it.

The Education Department State-Wide

This department has been cut to pieces. In the past three years, our unit at this prison has been decimated. All the schools within the system have had budget cuts. They are based on a three-year program, and by that time, all the departments in CDCR will be trimmed down even more due to state budget cuts. In our institution, we lost two librarians and two teachers by the end of February 2012. Around the same time, having no juniors below me played into why I felt that retirement was a good choice (in comparison to simply transferring to another institution).

Inmates and Education

For the entire sixteen years that I have been here, education for inmates has been a giant hoax. Yes, there is a need to have this program for someone with thirty years to life; they will reap the benefits on the street. It's all a make-work gig. Despite politics making the job more difficult than it has to, and it has been my wish for years for this to change, I am a realist and know nothing will. We have the potential to do good work here, but our hands are tied. We seem to inherit managers from other areas, such as Youth Authority, who have had great success with minors because there is a light at the end of the tunnel. With men in their middle ages, the story can be quite different. People came here to be teachers and managers, but had not a clue as to how the institution is run.

Another case of the square peg, round hole theory: due to the shrinking of positions, these teachers had to be placed somewhere, and here they are. Not to say that they are not very good teachers where they once were, but this is a different animal that has to take some time getting used to. The amount of mental stress working at the institution takes a toll on anyone. The bottom line: teachers at the prison work in an institution that is continually in a state of isolation, one teacher per classroom, which means that during the day my time is eaten up with that entity. The prep time we are supposed to have is almost nonexistent. We meet the first Wednesday of every month for a staff meeting with management, which is practically a wasted notion. We discuss the same things repeatedly every month, and there seems to be no answer—like trying to grab the ring on the merry-go-round ride when blindfolded. Like the teacher in school districts, we must deal with sloth, ignorance, and dumbness. I sometimes am amazed anything is accomplished at the institution.

The Custody vs. the Teacher Issue

Those who run the system are the correctional officers, and they know it. That teachers are on the lower end of the food chain is written in concrete. Again, officers think the teaching is a waste of time and that felons are lower than dirt. They ask, "Why educate them?" If they had kept their way, the inmates would be in their cells twenty-four hours a day. I have noticed for the most part that anytime an inmate asks an officer anything, they cannot wait to say no, dismiss him, or act as if he is too busy. Now having said this, there are many fine officers who do their job with style and professionalism and are to be applauded. Yet I do not realize security is the key that drives the institution, and I am not knocking it, but they should do their job and allow me to do mine. It is a truism that anyone who shows any kindness is looked at as being "over familiar" with the inmates, and yet, as a teacher, we have a job to be nurturing and compassionate.

I understand the rules have been taught to deal with all situations and not to cross the line of being over familiar. After all these years, I have noticed that, while I have tried to be friendly with officers, I have been pushed aside like I'm not even there, and have realized they have their own world, which excludes anyone outside of it. When inmates are locked down, the teachers try and play catch up: doing lesson plans and filing. To the officer we are doing nothing and being paid for it. It becomes almost sinister. Not only did I have to have two eyes to watch the inmates, but also, I need a third to watch everyone else. Anyone who's not in their clique is just a waste of time; after all, with a high school diploma they can make at least $100,000 in overtime.

Budgets

The state is broke. Let us do more cutbacks.

Classification

I'm still amazed that no matter how we try to have the correct inmate in the class, the ones who need the GED and those who already have one, it never happens that way. The policy is that once an inmate has a committee hearing he is placed on a list for education, vocation, or a work assignment. The committee decided where the inmate will be placed based on the needs of the institution. The inmate may have his GED/HS diploma in his file, but it is usually not there. The issue is that teachers who serve on the committee have a say but no input as to where the individual will be placed. If placed in education or on a waiting list, I check through the system to find out if he has a GED or any other documentation. Trying to get him reassigned is like trying to lance a boil on your ass: you just can't reach it. It usually takes anywhere from three months (if you're lucky) to six months to have the inmate go back to committee and be reassigned. Needless to say, this has been an uphill battle for years, and we wind up making enemies with the people in charge.

This also pisses off the inmate who has to precede the information, wants to get out of class, and gets stuck with me until I can get him out of class. It is a never-ending circle. Every principal has tried to remedy this issue and has fallen on their face. It is not going to happen. So we send out to different areas outside of the prison four, five times to get the documentation, and this becomes a round-robin all over again.

Finally, we could make the system work by modifying some of the items I have mentioned above. I do not want to create the wheel. I just want to see it fixed. This adventure could be made to work as long as everyone is on the same page, have no axes to grind, or have their own kingdoms. Perhaps an oversight committee or watchdog agency (like the Little Hoover Commission) could take a stand; this entire system will go down the rat hole. Maybe now is the time to do something more proactive.

My story has taken four years to write, and in reality, it has been a labor of love and a way to keep my sanity. I hope that I have not offended anyone too badly but just have stated my personal case. It is shared by others, hard to say. I hope that you have enjoyed it as much as I have had writing it. I am just one cog in the machine, nor am I a professional writer. I took this on as a whim to use this as a way of letting off steam and bringing awareness to these aforementioned issues.

Turning the Pages

I want the reader to understand that even though I am at odds with the way management works, I still have loved teaching in the prison system. My view of the insanity of the whole system keeps me sane, and indeed that can be considered a real paradox. The teacher must understand how the teacher/inmate culture works. As I have said, this culture is made of many ethnic groups—African American, Latino American, and White constituting the majority. Yes, there are splinter groups in each larger group, but the groups are the key players.

Since each group has its own sphere of influences, and to impose oneself onto another group is deemed disrespectful in the prison culture, tension between said-groups is always high. The disrespect inherent in such an act could and has led to physical altercations. The word respect is very important in this system. Everyone has to know where their place is in society, and to follow the inmate rules are much more important than the prison ones. The prison one can be avoided. The inmate rules, if not followed, can get you killed; inmates know these rules in order to stay alive.

From the teacher's point of view, culture is that of student learning. The most crucial function in the school is that of education and the student's progress in the attainment of the GED To me, there is nothing more satisfying than to have an inmate graduate. At the graduation ceremony, the student is outfitted with cap and gown, the family, press, and friends of the family are present at the event. This venue provides a positive action in a sea of depression. The student must know that time spent in the classroom has a purpose; such as the GED Students in this educational setting have difficulty when change occurs they may fear that when a favorite teacher is reassigned there will be problems with the new instructor. Misdirected change can result in confusion for them, especially when programs and policies are unclear to students, teachers, or anyone else.

The prison teacher's role is to change the student's perception that they are failures in the classroom. They are in prison because they have failed in society for such reasons as: discipline problems in school, gang activity and affiliation, broken families, no families, multiple addictions, being in and out of prison, and failure to conform in mainstream society. This permeates the air and students can wear it like a suit of clothes. The mindset has to be reworked so that a student can succeed if he wants to. The attitude must change from "I can't" to "I can." I have to make the student understand that here is where change can be made. The classroom provides the setting where learning will occur. The teacher has to act as the facilitator for all the students and guide them through their assignments. He may be paroled, his body will wither with age, but it has always been my belief that the mind must be used and that knowledge is power. I use the motto: "Give a man to fish and he will eat for a day. Teach him to fish and he will eat for a lifetime."

One must understand that, at Lancaster State Prison, the population of males generally comes from a poor or economically disadvantaged background. Without a doubt, the best way for males to grow, particularly in such in environment, is to have a role model who is also successful. This role model should be someone that a child can look up to or copy. In contrast, the "role models" at the prison are all bad; he inmate replicates those who have survived the system and made the best of it. In the harsh socioeconomic conditions of African and Hispanic American cultures there is normally no positive role model. As previously stated, inmates' home lives play integral roles in how these people have turned out.

Many gangs are formed on the basis of shared racial and ethnic backgrounds. All gangs in or out of prison are loyal to them, and anyone who gets in the way of their operations is the enemy. The criminal offender who is a gang member once incarcerated seeks members of his own tribe; and has his brothers and sisters to help him out. The new fish has someone who will teach him the ropes, supply him with the essential material needs until he can operate on his own, even though he has to pay a "kickback" to those above him, because they have provided the goods to get him started. And again, the shot caller's word is law; older inmates know the gang policy and rules by heart, where the freshly incarcerated are expected to know these tenants as quickly as possible. In most Latino gangs, the role is "blood in and blood out" the moment a young gang member is brought in. his loyalty is to that group and he will die to keep that group's integrity intact. The gang's orders are followed without question. If a member is ordered to kill another member or someone outside of the group and refuses, his life will be forfeited.

California prisons are the most violent in America. From 1981 =-1998, correctional officers killed over forty inmates during riots or major altercations, inmate on inmate, or inmates who have attacked staff. What this means is that the prison gangs make a conscience effort against correctional officers, and anyone else who gets in the way. Most of these gangs have a semi military structure and have developed their own way of life, culture, and economic system within the prison walls. Everyone—and I do mean everyone—has their own "hustle" to make money. Under these circumstances, how do I, as the teacher, make the point than an education is a viable tool to those who couldn't care less? Using a broad curriculum of educational skills and tools, the use of reading, writing, composition, language development, and the ability of being a circus barker to get their attention and keeping it is the best way to provide the services that the inmates need. My goal has always been to get into their heads. While I was always friendly with them, my goal was to help these people by becoming friends with them.

Providing the best services for my clientele has always been important to me and worked as a great motivator for the seventeen years that I worked at the prison. I don't BS the inmates, nor do I shine them on. What occurs, instead, is a symbiotic relationship: I have an interest in them, and they have one in me. I act like a showman, and my goal is to get the best out of them. Not only do I want them to give an answer to the question, but also I want them to know how they got that answer. I try and go beyond. I want them to think and to be able to see the "light go on." When that happens, it is all work it, or when a student says, "I finally get it." That is worth more than gold to me. Getting into the students' heads is one of the keys to becoming a worthy educator. Plus, it has the added benefit of getting a better understanding of what the student needs and wants out of the class. In other words, it creates a win-win situation. I like to create a synergy in the room. I always flew around the room with my coffee cup in my hand. The students joke and ask if the coffee should be taken away from him. All this is good, as the energy keeps the class focused and we are able to accomplish a great deal, creating a level playing field on which I treat all students as an educational equal who can learn freely without being chained by their pasts. In this way, students realize there are educational spaces in which they can expect honesty and trust. Such a benefit aids normal society. In the prison, it can potentially give someone wings.

But of course, accomplishing this is still a feat. Inmates can be strong defeatists. It's so hard for them to believe in themselves when their brains have been fired on everything and when their sense of self-worth has been so battered that to pull them from the trenches has required all the effort and resources at my disposal. We have used handheld video equipment to have the students role-play job interviews, what to ask on interviews, and how to deal with questions about their incarceration. There is no longer a reentry program at this facility. Working with how to deal with life skills is just as important as adding two and two, and I find that you can't have one without the order in order to have these students succeed.

The classroom, my classroom, is a space I consider as a center for learning. But when budget problems throughout the States caused our education department to have no money for texts, pencils, paper, and pens, it makes things rather difficult. I photocopied and did the consumable books that allowed me to fulfill my teaching needs. I purchased material that I needed in good times and bad because the material was needed for me to do my job. I didn't purchase material just to get a tax write-off. Most teachers learn to think on their feet and to have the ability to adapt, survive, and change at a moment's notice. Some of them are the following:

1. High expectations from all learners
2. Actively engaging students in the learning experience
3. Small group work with a structured format
4. Accountability of students
5. Multimedia instruction to facilitate auditory skills

As well as many other tools.

Like those exceptional teachers in the real world, I've become my own educational supply and procurement center.

Those who live more normal lives, the mainstream of society, constantly wonder why convicts keep coming back to prison. For the past fifteen years, I have often wondered, "What is the magnet that brings them back year after year?" It's certainly not the food or the accommodations. These men follow a daily routine from dawn to dusk, twenty-four hours a day, seven days a week, year in and year out. The routine is never-changing, of course—breakfast is full of monotony, along with the other regular daily activities. If an inmate is lucky to be a clerk and work in PIA (Prison Industries) and be paid anywhere from nine cents to sixty-five an hour, that job is usually done extremely well. So here is the problem. If an inmate can do a task well here, why not back in the real world? Sure, in jail they are a captive agent, but what about when released and on parole? I'm not a shrink, but ever wonder if even the inmates have the answer?

Let me give you an example of an inmate. Benito was a trustee, and he makes the magnificent sum of nineteen cents per hour. He is thirty-three years old, a person of a Californian Hispanic background. He was a gang member for most of his life. On his current "vacation," he had been incarcerated for fifteen years and required another five before being paroled. Ben started his schooling with the system, with Juvenile Hall. He was a "validated member" with Los Nortes from Northern California; what one would call a "Hermano" and was somewhat high in that organization. This could be called a "made man" in the mafia. His mother was a drug user, and his father was in the system as well. At the tender age of ten, he was selling drugs. He acquired his GED at the Folsom California State Prison and some college units from other prisons. Ben removed himself from the gang affiliation and, in dropping a dime on them, gave the prison officers all the information they didn't have about northern gangs. All right, so he snitched them out on the "Sensitive Need Yard" (where all other unaffiliated drug debtors and snitches are sent). He had been my trustee for almost a year when I hoped, aloud to myself, that I would have him until the end of my employment. He was a great worker and as loyal as he could be to me. I frequently pondered on what, if he had a normal life, what he could have done.

The drug culture impacts the poorer inner city communities, pulling innocents into a lifetime of crime like a moth to a flame at the prospect of improving their lives. Young men from such communities make up about 70 percent of the prison population. The sale of drugs becomes the economic basis for the community. Drugs provide easy and fast money for the dealer on the street corner but a risk of lifetime incarceration when one considers how such acts often correlate with violence. The person is usually a gang member, and being arrested for possession is not a problem, just a cost of doing business. The individual will be sent to an institution where he will be welcomed with open arms by a member of his family, gang or both, who are already there.

Society believes that inmates "should be seen and never heard from again." Prison is built far away from polite society, somewhere in the form of a leper colony; one touch at the average citizen is contaminated. The average Joe perceives that the inmate should be in a bare cell with a passport, bread, and water—and that's it. The public thinks that inmates have it too good with TVs, education, and free movies. Inmates purchase almost all items that the state does not require. They pay for their own televisions (purchased from one company only to pay about 60 percent more). Movies are rented from the inmate welfare fund. These movies have to have a PG rating. When visitation day comes, the inmate's families are gouged by the vending machines in the visiting areas; the family needs to have a minimum of twenty dollars in quarters, and that can quickly be used up.

From Civvies to Dress Blues

What has changed in the prison system? Almost nothing, for the guy or girl who gets caught with their hand in the cookie jar. When the employee becomes careless and thinks "I'll only bend the rules" once, it leads into trouble quite quickly. It may be close to Christmas, Thanksgiving, your birthday, or even an inmate's birthday—it doesn't matter. When an inmate asks you to bring in little favors, which are almost insignificant, you tell yourself, "Just once, no one will ever know." You start small—snacks, magazines—and then the hook is set in your mouth.

In reality, that "small thing" has become cell phones, chargers, iPads, and even drugs. So the inmates who have been your buddy will now reel you in. You tell yourself it started small, and then you might have gotten away with it, but those days are long gone. You tell yourself this can't be happening; I've worked ten, twelve, nineteen years in the system and never mis-stepped. Well, in for a penny, in for a pound. You've watched all the training films on being over familiar with inmates for years and never thought this would happen to you. You've seen many people "walked off" the facility and wondered how they could give up a career for very little money.

I had a close friend fired. She was involved in a cigarette deal with an inmate. She told me she had to do it because she gave him blow jobs and if not he would report her. I told her I would save her job and lose a friend. I reported it, and she paid a monetary fine for over two years. She was finally fired later on for having phone sex with inmates.

Inmates have all the time in the world to watch you. They listen to your conversations with colleagues. They know what you like and don't like. They are a giant ear, and whatever they pick up from you, that information is shared with other cons. As diligent as they were in watching me, I was just the same in watching them.

I once had an inmate who asked me where I lived, I told him the San Fernando Valley. I had lived there for twenty years. I knew he was fishing for information. He wanted to know if I knew different places, which I did. I could see how he tried to work me. In reality, I gave nothing away and worked him. I played with him for years. I knew the valley like my hand.

I knew many people in my career who were never going to get caught. They were too smart, but not smart enough. What tripped those employees up was that there was always someone smarter than them. There are always the employees that are looking for the quick buck and your buddy; the inmates will give you up to authorities if you don't fulfill your end of the bargain. What do I mean by giving you up? Simple. When the inmate has gotten all that he can get from you, he's used you up, he will tell the authorities what you have done for him.

What will happen to the inmate? He will be sent to administrative segregation (the hole) for a few months, lose privileges and canteen for a while. He will then be back on the yard looking for another patsy. Very little happens to him, but a lot is going to happen to you. (If I sound bitter or sarcastic, it is meant to be.) I took too many people handcuffed and removed them from the facility. The employee can forget his pension plan. He or she will have to explain to family and friends the life you knew is over. If you go to prison, you'll be placed in protective custody and maybe get a job for eighteen cents an hour. You'll never get another job, and the job that was given up was for peanuts.

The Cream Sinks and the
Shit Floats to the Top

This chapter of the book covers the mental acumen, or lack thereof, and how people with no skills rise to their level of incompetence. After my years at the prison as teacher, I have come to the conclusion that if a brain-eating fungus came inside, then it would starve to death. We have had managers who reached this position through no fault of their own. Any skills that they learned along the way of being a teacher were quickly forgotten when they moved up. Their brain cells were erased by supervision.

Anyone who expects to be a vice principal has come to complete the master's program in education administration, either write a thesis or take an exam to prove they have the skills to be a supervisor. The program is well taught by professors who know their craft. Too many people, however, pass these tests, earn the job, and eventually become a pain in the ass. They do not truly care for the cause. Their number one interest is themselves, their income, and any promotions they may encounter by following or exploiting the rules. All the others strive for the pot of gold for their own gratification. They are not team players and are inherently selfish. And so, teaching such individuals proves especially useless when they entirely ignore what they've supposed to learn and become extremely difficult to work with. Not to be negative, we do have personnel who went through this program and are exceptions to the rule, as has been previously mentioned. But in terms of truly fixing the inmate issues at hand, their participation makes general operation harder.

Without a doubt, their selfishness lowers the real potential of societal impact. By using the simple tools I have discussed in the overview, a poor or indifferent supervisor could become competent. But naturally, ego gets in the way.

For instance, teachers have caused problems simply under the premise that their input should be regarded above anyone else's. Group meetings go nowhere when all the teachers involved can't seem to come up with one course of action, one solution, to whichever problem they might have had to deal with at the time. Therefore, constant conflict among teachers and almost always present, carrying over the span of months and slowing down operations. Nothing really even gets done. This effect has a demoralizing way of making the rest of us who do want to do the job that much harder. What occurs is that the caboose is pushing the engine instead of the other way around. Sometimes I believe that those who do a professional job should manage the managers. Most schools operate by a vision statement. For many years we had one, however, in the last six or seven years, that has gone down the drain. This, a think quite solidly, will be improved with a new vision statement.

A vision statement is important to any school. It is created to set the standards and goals that are published and presented to the entire school population. Once we had a one, but it never came to fruition. It had affirmations that all agree to sign off on, such as "This school will have at least two hundred students and achieve their GED by the end of the school year." It was simple enough. The job is spelled out as to how that will be done and who will be given specific tasks to accomplish this. The staff was then encouraged to buy into the plan and was on board. Indeed, this vision statement would have been placed in each classroom with the school goal posted therein, but this never happened—an unfortunate occurrence since this school policy could have been a living document for the institution, with material that can be added and deleted, all depending on the wants, needs, and desires of the school community.

In our school, most of the teachers would have really liked a system like this. Somehow, instead of the plan becoming a reality, it just went away and never came back. We do the talk but not the walk. Consider this thing as a hand with five fingers that wiggle. Each finger is independent of the others and do not work in unison. We are that hand. If all the fingers would work together as a handle, then we would be quite strong. Instead, the system I work in is the wiggly one and is dysfunctional at best. We the shareholders must have precise and clear understanding of what management want, yet management has no clear idea of what they want. What we lack from supervision is motivation, honesty, and enthusiasm. We need people above us who can capture our hearts and minds to make those of us who are exceptional go the 110 percent and feel even more enthusiastic about their jobs and their possible impact.

I have found that the students come to the realization that they can do the work successfully and have the solution to material that he has never attempted before. Some of the items that we use are the following:

1. Classrooms should be showcases of learning—with books, posters, and inmate work pasted to the walls
2. Engaging students in the learning modality
3. Use issue of the day, TV, and all appropriate tools
4. Make the students accountable for the work, then express self-pride in what they do.
5. Enjoying the job that we do and the inmates understand that we care and are professional, making the job even more rewarding to us all.

I have included samples of educators, one that falls into the ideal category and another which falls far under expectations.

The first is "Doc." He is one of the finest educators that I have ever known. He came to the prison system with over thirty years of educational experience, most of that in management. He never tripped over his ego, and working with him was like a breath of fresh air. He had an interest in the students, and they in the method of his teaching. It was all done without the use of bullshit. He made a success of these classes. Understand that he did not walk on water. He was just a mortal like you and me whose efforts have made a positive impact on inmate lives. He and I had the same outlook on getting the job accomplished, treating these students like people, and they appreciated that we cared about them.

The second is a teacher who was self-gratifying, untrustworthy, a liar and thief who pissed off everyone he made contact with. In the fourteen years that he was at this prison, he made himself the center of the universe. In my life I have never found a vainer, more self-absorbed person with no skills and fewer social graces. According to him, he had been an IRS agent, a lieutenant commander in the Navy, a lawyer, a CIA agent, the butcher, the baker, the candlestick maker. According to him, the only friends that he had were the inmates. He was a success about talking about himself and taking credit for what others had accomplished. One of his greatest skills was brownnosing management about how great he was and we were not. This sink of humanity was promoted twice to the vice principal slot at two different prisons.

We thought that we were well able to get rid of him, but that did not happen. He managed to screw up both times and was demoted to teacher, and they sent him back to our prison as punishment for us. We finally were able to get rid of him when all the teacher cuts occurred. He was told for his best interest that he should transfer to another institution—he would be high enough on their seniority list and therefore would not be cut from the system. This plan was put into place, and that was the last we heard from him. Amen. We understand what they want and how to make the system work.

People like this appear to go around and around day in and day out, and those who are in charge have little clue as to what goes on or how the job is supposed to work or function.

What causes this is that we have two categories of character here. The first group I have chosen to call the floaters. The floaters are teachers and managers, as I mentioned before, who do very little just to get by and are happy with a paycheck. They waste class time, my time, by working rumors about who got more than they did in the way of reward. They are never satisfied, showing a lack of productivity, and everyone else is to blame for their lack of effort. They are entitled by the system from the cradle to the grave.

As mentioned, instead of teaching by using the tools in their room, they would rather give the students handouts as they read the paper. They prefer to

1. not to be a part of anything;
2. do little to improve the school;
3. have no interest in building a school community, but rather to tear it down;
4. it's always about them and their needs; and
5. they deal with self-preservation and barely function.

Basically, success is not an option.

On the other hand, we have the second group: the doers. They have a completely different approach, of course, and will hopefully be the ones to continue providing helpful services to inmates, negating all the bad of selfish professionals like the person described above. These students who are taught by caring people know that we have a vested interest in their success, and it shows by their test scores.

Anatomy of a Setup

Working in the system is more than just teaching. It's your head above water and watching out for pitfalls that can have you collared, removed from your position, and fired. The first week in the system, all employees go through an orientation period of how, who, and where the system works for our benefit. This class kept me in a good stead while working there.

The inmates in the system have all day to watch us, to listen to what we say and whom we talk to, because they have nothing but time. Every little piece of information can be used, and after all the inmates want to be our friends so that later they can blackmail us into bringing in contraband. They can be used sometime down the road. For instance, I may have to write up an inmate for an infraction and he might say to me, "Lockshin, you're really a great teacher, and you know I do all the work, and this is the first time you were going to write me up, why don't you let this one go?"

"OK, I'll let it go this time."

The following week:

"Lockshin, I'm an artist, could you let me have a few mechanical pencils?"

Later on:

"Thanks for the pencils. You know I could use a sketchbook and they don't sell them in the store. Could you get one for me and I'll do your portrait for free? Besides, no one will even know. They might have them at Wal-Mart."

So now the hook has been set, I allowed him to get away with an infraction, and now I've become his art supplier. It gets better.

"The sketchbook is great, but I'm in trouble. I need a favor. I have a gambling debt, and the only way out of it without being stabbed is if I give them five packs of cigarettes."

"Can't do it," I'd tell them.

"OK, but you know, I could tell the cops that you brought stuff in for me and it will be your job."

"OK, you'll have it tomorrow."

Game. Set. Match.

As you can see, the hook has been swallowed, and I'm caught. Even though against my better judgment, I allowed myself to become compromised. The inmate will squeeze me like a lemon, and when he has used me, he'll tell the authorities anyway, and there goes the job, and he gets sent to the hole for five months.

While this never really happened, it's an example as to what could and does happen all the time. People get caught in all situations and do one of three things:

1. They tell no one and hope to ride it out.
2. They tell on themselves and hope to keep their job (and perhaps be fined for twenty-four months).
3. Be given up by the inmate and lose a $60,000–$80,000 job for chump change.

If you don't go to jail, you can kiss any municipal job goodbye. You would be surprised how many civilians, officers, cooks, nurses, and free staff have been "walked out" of the institution for doing this—all because of a little money gain and sheer stupidity. I find it amazing that people could throw away a job and career for no money. The advantage or mind-set is that they will never get caught, but they always do. Go tell your wife and kids that you're fired from a state job and may have to be a greeter at Wal-Mart from now on.

The two largest items of contraband that are smuggled in are drugs and cell phones. The price of a cell phone in the prison goes between $600 and $900 per phone. The battery charger is extra. In 2010, correctional officers throughout the entire prison system confiscated over 11,000 cell phones, and that's over thirty-three prisons.

That's a lot of money. The risks are great, but the profitability is very high. In 2010, the penalty for any employee found guilty of bringing in such material would be a felony as well as being fired.

Drugs, the second largest item of smuggled contraband, have always been a problem in the system. There is major money that can be made here, usually by the Mexican mafia, found in northern institutions (such as San Quentin, Folsom, and Pelican Bay). The leaders of this group, even though incarcerated, have a long reach throughout the system. Ever since I've been at Lancaster, drugs have been a thriving business. On visiting day, the wives of inmates arrived and usually give their spouses a kiss. In some cases, that tongue is pushing small balloons of coke into their husband's mouth where it is swallowed and retrieved later. At the end of the visit, the inmate will go back to his cell, have a bowel movement, pass the balloons through the anal tract and is now ready for business. Of course, the inmate is searched before he returns to his cell.

Sometimes the guards get lucky. If an inmate is suspected of swallowing this material, he is placed in a cell in the infirmary that has an enmeshed toilet. The inmate is now on "potty watch." Two things may happen at this point. The inmate may pass the bundles of material out into the mesh container, or in the worst case, the bundle dissolves due to the digestive juices of the stomach. Here, the inmate is in trouble because he might overdose. However, before that were to happen, his stomach would be pumped out. In the toilet scenario, the inmate is constantly watched until the drug material passes through. In these situational instances, like any other contraband, the case is adjudicated, and he is sent to the hole for a period of time. To be quite candid, the inmate may be caught, but to him, the risks taken and the money to be made are well worth it. Remember, if the inmate is serving a twenty-five, fifty, or life sentence, four or five months in the hole is well worth it and no big deal.

The thought of doing anything illegal never entered my mind. To spend jail time in a jail with "Bubba" did not agree with me. The idea of losing my job, the shame and stigma to my family was never appealing, and yet, over all the years, there it happened to others all the time. Inmates would always ask me for favors. I told them, "I don't do favors. I take requests." They knew that I was not going to allow myself to be placed in any situation. They also knew I respected them, and they me, and we kept the relationship on a professional basis. An example of this was during my first year (1996). My class asked me what I could charge them to bring in a pizza. I told them $1,000,000 dollars, as I would need an income when I got fired. They then asked about two pizzas, and I told them the amount doubled.

I was allowed to bring in material as long as it was approved by the prison. Usually, books I would get from friends or the library, and I would have to have a donation letter signed by the appropriate authority and a record of what I brought in. This was to protect them and myself. So that you understand, I was never going to be a victim of a setup. I realized that I had to look at myself in the mirror each night and had to be honest with myself. I never allowed myself to be tripped up by this.

The Men Who Stare at Goats
(or Stare at Nothing at All)

M y partner Willie gave me the inspiration for this section of the book. We think it's an appropriate title for the section. Let me bring you, the reader, up to date. I believe that I mentioned this, the Bridging Program, back in January 2010. Like the Titanic it had sunk down the drain of the state. It had left few survivors, and the wise ones at Sacramento had decimated the education department of thirty-three prisons across the state. The vocational teachers of all these institutions had circled that drain and were finally flushed out. For that matter, few of the academic teachers were spared. Out of a department staff of sixty-two, fifty were expunged.

Between January and April 2010, those of us who had seniority sat and stared at each other wondering what we were going to do, waiting for Sacramento to come up with a viable plan. Sitting around with nothing to do is no fun and makes time go by slowly. We didn't have goats to stare at, only each other, and truly, that was no bargain. A few of us decided to make up an educational material, duplicate it, and use the copies in the prison housing units.

The rumors were like assholes. Everyone knew one. We were informed by Sacramento that we would be teaching again. The mental giants who had forgotten how to teach came up with a modular program. These programs work in the following manner. Each teacher would have 125 students per week: twelve in the morning (7:00 a.m.–10:00 a.m.) and twelve in the afternoon (11:00 a.m.–2:00 p.m.). We would have each group for three hours per day. For example, group A would come in on Monday from 7:00 a.m. to 10:00 a.m., and we would not see them again until the following Monday. We would also supply them with twelve hours of homework that they would do in their cells and return it on the following class day.

Like the inmate buildings are a place to study. I taught GED, and instead of twelve per session, I usually had an average of eight. In reality, I should have had the same inmates every day, not just one time per week per class. The state in its wisdom has decided otherwise. During the start-up period, I was housed on the C Yard. It was locked down for six weeks during this time period. The cause of this lockdown was a sit-down strike, because equipment in the show area was dirty and substandard. Over six hundred inmates took part in this strike. From May 2010 to mid-June 2010, we did nothing. The taxpayers paid me to sit as we were not allowed to go to the building to provide materials to our students. However, I made my time valuable by copying everything and anything that would help me in the classroom. Facility C has never been a programming yard. In other words, things did not run smoothly there. Things are always in flux.

Custody never seem to learn from the same mistakes that are made over and over again. People should be able to do their job in a professional manner. If they would learn from their errors, we would have an opportunity to make advances, even in lockdown. The amazing thing is that some officers have an "I don't care" manner toward the inmates. They will do their job, but couldn't care less what happens. Their attitude is that safety and security are the only important factors, and so they should be. However, the guards have an attitude that becomes almost mind-numbing, a kind of robotic state where the job can be done by rote memory.

This attitude becomes first nature to the officers, yet when an inmate is injured, or has a life-threatening emergency, officers quickly provide a response. The incident, whatever it is, is rapidly concluded. However, on a day-to-day basis, most officers will do the job with as little effort as possible. The inmate is just a tool to an end, and that is the officer's paycheck and overtime.

Regarding teachers and the education department, most officers have the belief that it is a waste of money to provide inmates any tools of an education or anything else, especially those inmates who have life sentences. The overall belief is that people come to prison not for the first time (and one would think that a one-time stay in this system would be more than enough for anyone). People surely don't come here for the food or accommodations. And yet, they return over and over again. Officers believe that this in/out mentality will never change. Ironically enough, both groups suffer from what I call the "institutionalized syndrome." Officer or inmate—it didn't matter. Both sounded like the same person.

When referring to this similarity as a syndrome, I mean to say that each group is practically a mirror image of each other. Both sides can be mean, nasty, and annoying. I have mentioned before that we are constantly on a merry-go-round, repeating tendencies constantly. The custody side of the house has always thought that the teachers have the Stockholm syndrome. That we, the teachers, are always on the side of the inmates (especially when it comes to education and having them get to class on time). Officers are on the side of overtime. The part that is most troubling is that the officers have always believed that teachers are not necessary, whether they say this overtly or think it. Throughout my years having taught there, I have held the attitude that these people don't see us. They look right by us as if we don't exist. The guards would rather have the inmates locked down twenty-three hours a day with one hour for exercise. Almost like the zoo. People could come by and throw peanuts!

There is a second comment made by people at the institution whom are not teachers, but talk about teachers stating that we make too much money. My answer has always been the following, "We would teach for nothing. It is the stupidity we deal with on a daily basis that's the reason why we are not being paid enough!" When the yards are locked down, the officers have to cell feed: they go from cell to cell, providing the inmates with their meals, providing escort when inmates have to go to the infirmary or anywhere else. Once these tasks are done, the officers seem to disappear until the end of their shift.

There is an opinion that the Department of Corrections has become one giant wasteland. And by that I mean that those at the top of the chain have no clue or have forgotten what it is like to work in a correctional setting. We, those in Sacramento who have no clear understanding of what the institutional needs are or what we teachers do at the institution, work in a bureaucratic fog. An example of pure waste, as I have mentioned, is during all the past lockdowns. The inmates could have been brought to the education building, under escort, giving the teachers the opportunity to do the job that they are paid for. Having said this, I also understand that education is the weak sister, and that safety and security is the prime mission statement, which I totally agree with. Still, once the searches are concluded, education should resume in some format. During lockdowns, as I have said before, I made thousands of copies of materials to be used by the students so that I am prepared for students once the education privilege is restored. Consider the money I've made per hour as an office clerk, making copies, when my time could be made more useful to the students. With all the time spent on lockdowns, management here has the genius to ask how to make students prepared for the GED

Management thinks small or doesn't think at all. My class was locked down for weeks on end; no learning, three hours a week when they are here. They'll ask me, "How many students are prepared for the GED?" The right question should have been, "When will they be ready?" since, clearly, the lockdown stopped, paused their progress. At one management meeting, Principal Sir Lancelot told us that another institution had completed over three hundred GEDs (while Lancaster had none). My belief is that management wants quantity over quality. A new Sacramentans mantra, "Good for Pelican Bay," provides milestones, giving inmates up to six weeks off when they come up for parole (provided that they pass the GED). The caveat for this is that inmates cannot be lifers, nor have two strikes on their record. Among a list of 120 inmates on my roll, none qualified for this program.

The Return of the Two Thousand-Year-Old Man

T he system never ceases to amaze me. Let me explain. As of July 2012, there were ten teachers as educational staff at Lancaster prison. Due to budgetary cuts, we lost over sixty-five teachers the last few years. Some of these losses were due to retirement, staff being transferred to keep jobs, and losses due to teachers not having enough time in the state service to be kept on—a real bloodbath. Those with less than five years' service were farmed out. They got jobs at 30 percent less or looked for position outside the system. Those not involved with the educational slaughter across the state couldn't have cared less, for it did not mean anything to them. Yet the world does change, and three of the teachers with less than five years were brought back to this prison and reinstated. One of the teachers coming back would be who I call the "two-thousandyear-old man."

This person had worked as a teacher for about three years while we were working on the now-defunct Bridging Program. Some jobs are contained the old-fashioned way: they blackmail the people who would hire them. The rumor was that he was a man over the retiree age and told those who interviewed him that if he were not employed he would sue for age discrimination.

With this information, he was then hired to avoid a lawsuit. He should have remained retired; he had served in World War II and couldn't remember it. A nicer man you will not find, but in this dangerous world, he was in over his head. He was totally inept in the prison environment. The more he was taught, the less that was retained. It was like trying to keep water in a colander; it just can't be done. We all knew this person was over his head and mentioned our concerns to management. They analyzed our concerns and told us to mind our own business. He would leave for one building on the yard and arrive at another; our concern is that we did not know where he was. Understand that it's very important here to know where people are at all times. It's the best part of security, just in case of emergencies, lockdowns, or inmate riots. Security trumps everything.

I had explained this fact to him because a few years back, a teacher had been killed at Chino State Prison. Her body had been dumped in a garbage dumpster, and no one knew where she was for three days. I used this story as an example as to what could happen to him and made it crystal clear. It only got worse, although he tried to do the best that he could. Luckily for him and us, his seniority was low with the department, and he was given a job outside the prison. Unfortunately, he's been reinstated with the prison system since then. I wish him the best of luck.

Disability and the Medal of Honor

We all know that in the military, the Medal of Honor is the highest achievement a person can obtain for bravery, for going above and beyond the call of duty. In the prison system, there, too, is such an achievement: going out on disability (of course, I'm being facetious here). These people, too, face certain dangers like hangnails, falling, getting hit by a door, running an electrical cart into a wall, or just being scared by a mouse. These dangers also have certain amounts of time off that a person can obtain. It's obvious that a hangnail won't get you much time, but it's a start.

Going out on stress is the highest award that a state employee can achieve because it is difficult to clearly define. A misspoken word, a comment, or glance—the things might put someone right over the top. I'm not knocking the claims that are legitimate, but there are certain groups of people who know the ins and outs of disability and could more than likely do a seminar on it. We use vacation or sick time when you can just fall down. Follow me and I'll give a few examples.

The first is a teacher who shall, for these purposes, be called Madame Butterfly. She had been married three or four times, and one day in her classroom, an inmate exposed himself (pulled out his Johnson). Granted, this was a serious inmate infraction, and the inmate was sent to the hole. Madame Butterfly was struck dumb by this experience but had seen enough Johnsons to last a lifetime. She went on stress for six months. However, during this interlude, she was not too stressed out to finish her master's degree.

The second is a teacher whom I have known for over sixteen years. At the time of this occurrence, this person has had eighteen years of state service, and about ten years of that service has been out on disability. I have never known a person who has enjoyed being out of work for one affliction or another and relishes in talking about them with great gusto like they do. This individual, when she returns to work, could be like a bionic person and should be held in awe for the amount of time she has been out of work.

Understand that there are legitimate cases of persons who are truly injured for whatever reason with some sort of disability, and I am not criticizing them. It's all the others who take advantage of the system. We, the public, are paying for it. These folks use this time off as an interlude from work, and it doesn't even bother them. I was once on disability. I was injured due to an eighteen-hour surgery on my back. It was fused, causing me to be out for eighteen months. I was told that state investigators would secretly videotape my comings and goings. I couldn't have cared less. I wore a thirty-pound back brace, and they could have filmed to their hearts' content. I had nothing to hide. There were meetings with a state shrink who went over my case and asked if I wanted to retire on half pay. After being home all the time, I wanted to go back to work. He really thought I was crazy but signed off my return work status. It could have been a free ride, but I would not take it and would rather be working than sitting home and talking to the dog.

So we come to the crux of reality. I've come to the conclusion that a good many people are honest and have integrity and do a professional job for a fair wage. However, there are those who will work the system for all they can get out of it. There are also those people who look with awe and jealousy to those who would work the disability system.

The Inmates on the Honor Yard

From 2000 to 2004 and 2010 to 2012, I was the assigned GED teacher on the A Yard, which was the Honor Yard at Lancaster State Prison. In the year 2000, this yard started out as an experiment to how an honor yard should be run. This was and is to my knowledge the only yard designated as an honor yard in the state system. To be assigned to this yard, inmates have to be discipline-free. That is, no infractions for at least five years, and second, no known gang affiliations. It has to be a total programming yard, which means that any program, education, vocation class, library, or prison industry has to continuously run in a smooth operational format.

On this yard, one would find inmates in all sorts of productive activities: inmates teaching others how to play musical instruments, peer education classes, managing budgets, how to work in the real world, and a host of others. These programs do not cost the state and the public one time. Most of the funds come from sales to other inmates. These sales take the form of food normally and whatever profit that is used to keep the programs running. Say, for example, materials that cannot be obtained on the side can be purchased elsewhere. Since this concept was introduced, the inmates have used two classrooms for multiple purposes in the education building.

Over 3,700 inmates have been involved in these programs since 2004, without a single incident. These rooms are used by inmates who want to learn the following: how to be better writers, dealing with anger management, being better husbands and fathers, how to deal with life, and how to be a better person if and when paroled. They use these classes to make the most of their time behind bars, instead of talking the yard day in and day out. The inmate peer instructors were given the privilege of doing this program, which by all rights was a success. These peer inmates also work with teacher volunteers, public volunteers, public volunteers, and others who provide sponsorship to this program. I also provided support to this, giving my time freely and helping the warden. It was a pleasure to be able to help in any way I could to make this program workable. The brainchild for the program came from dedicated teachers, other staff, and help from the Department of Corrections in Sacramento. The mandate was to

1. "afford each person committed to the custody of the Director of Corrections every reasonable opportunity and encouragement to participate in rehabilitative activities. In addition, that a consistent effort be made to ensure the effectiveness of the treatment of these programs."
2. "whether in attending the many activities given or by sharing the knowledge and expertise to reach out in addition, train others under the supervision, and or any authorized employee."

There have been those individuals at Lancaster prison who for years wished that this program would fail, go away, or both. The attitude is that inmates don't need to be educated, or have any type of constructive organization because they are in prison to be punished and that should be the end of it. For many years, this program has hung on a thread of being cancelled, yet progressive minds in Sacramento believe that a program like this should be kept alive. Even some of the detractors begrudgingly see that it works rather well. There will always be a control issue. Custody is always aware that issues might happen, and their concern is important, yet that issue of problems has never reared its ugly head.

The public needs to know that within these confined walls there is success for inmates using their own resources. If you said "Big deal, why didn't they do this before being incarcerated?" you would be right. Inside, there is time for reflection and the ability to change. HBO has filmed on this Honor Yard many times to get the flavor as to how well this works. If this program could be cloned and used elsewhere, maybe recidivism syndrome would be reduced. Is it not possible for people to change after being incarcerated for fifteen, twenty years of life without parole? I, too, believed that in all the public stereotypes of prison, but working there had changed my point of view. Sure, there are many inmates who need to stay here for the rest of their life; however, there are those who are worthy of a second chance. I, for one, know that I am not the same person I was twenty-five years ago, nor are you.

The Death of the Golden Goose

I've worked at the institution from 1996 to 2012. I have never worked at another institution, nor do I know how other places are run and organized. I can only write about this one.

We have had many state governors: Wilson, Dukemajian, Davis, "the Terminator," and Brown, who pandered to the Correction Officers Union. Over sixteen years, this union was able to get pay raises for its membership due to their lobby in Sacramento. While they reaped in the benefits of these raises, many other bargaining units never got any, just the golden finger and those who are starved to death. Those other units never had the clout that the officers union had. So the cash rolled in year after year. Indeed, the union gave a great deal of money to those running for governor so that the well would never run dry.

Many officers that I knew came to Lancaster prison not because it was a premiere showcase, which it was not, but because it gave them the opportunity to make a great deal of money by achieving the limit of fifteen days of overtime. Imagine someone with a high school diploma or GED who enters a world where they would make $100,000 a year and more (picture a sea of green uniforms, like penguins, marching as a group, yelling, "Overtime, overtime"). This became the main topic of their conversations. They lived and thirsted to get as much of the cash pie as they could. Some officers made over $200,000 per year, and that was because they were almost living at the prison. This money was almost like manna from heaven. Oh, how the money for them poured in. I can remember that I did not get a raise for five years, but they never missed out. The more they made, the more they wanted.

When Corrections Corporation of America was planning to build private prisons, the Correction Officers Union almost had a stroke. How dare someone else get this money? It was like taking the food out of their mouth. They squeezed their lobbyist in Sacramento to put an end to such a plan, but to no avail. The private entity was allowed to proceed. The union had its hand on the pulse of the prison. After inmates were cell fed and their cells checked during lockdowns that lasted weeks, officers would sit in a small office and camp out. To them, having a yard locked down was like a blessing, requiring less work out of them and causing less headaches overall.

During the early stages of the prison cuts, other departments such as education were bled white, and they could not care less as long as they were sage. The wheel does tum sometimes. With the state circling the money drain, it implemented a series of cuts that would affect all state employees. In June 2012, it was mandated that retirement, seniority, or officers finding work at other institutions would reduce the correctional officer force. For about ten years, they have had it their own way. Some officers even told me those times have changed and that the good times would soon be over, that they had done it to themselves by being too greedy. Time will tell as to what will happen in the future.

Through the Looking Glass

I f you thought my/your confusion was over, try again. Despite the many times this book has been written, I always find more things to say, and really, this shouldn't come as a surprise. I have become "Alice," and the CDC has become "wonderland."

In June 2012, my associate Kelly was transferred from yard to D Yard, which meant that I was going to be the only teacher on a yard. Not only was I going to teach GED, but also work with her two classes of developmentally disabled students. So now I would have to teach four classes in two different rooms at the same time. I'm good, but not that good. My two GED classes would be kaput, and I would have to keep the best students of her classes to make one class. Confused yet? No one in management had the foresight to figure out how I was supposed to handle four classes, nor did they want to.

I decided that I would be the one who would make all the decisions because no one else wanted to. Therefore, if I failed, I would be the one who would get all the blame. With the help of my good friend in inmate assignment, we were able to create two classes from four. This was completed with the approval of the inmate assignment lieutenant as well as my own in order to make it work. Doing it in this format, it came off without a hitch. The next step was the classroom.

I had a very small classroom, and the one next door was twice the size. Plus, it had the advantage that it was air-conditioned. There is nothing worse, in the high desert, especially in the summer, than being in a room with twenty-nine inmates and the smell of rotting feet and behinds permeating thickly in the air. So clearly, a room with air-conditioning was an added bonus. I was told I could be moving my material from one class to the other and still teach both at the same time. I told her this was impossible and that I would close my class for two days and get everything moved. I got it done in a day in a half.

At our monthly staff meeting, our "Queen Mum" talks and we listen, period. There is no discussion unless we agree with her because she does not want to hear anything we have to say. She feels superior of such managerial skills. On July 27, 2012, we were going to have a GED graduation. Most of the students who would partake came from my class and someone who I shall refer to as "Mr. Hollywood." She asked for volunteers for the graduation, and so I did. I was asked to price cake and balloons, which we would have in one of the visiting areas. Someone else would handle the committee for the program. I got all the prices, and at the last minute, we were told that "Queen Mum" decided she would do it herself. In other words, I had been kicked to the curb. Other teachers called me to ask what was needed, as I was co-chair for this.

"Don't you know what's going on? You're in charge."

"I'm only partly in charge and have not been told anything."

As a matter of fact, neither "Mr. Hollywood" nor I were noted in the program that was presented to those who attended. Like a slap in the face. I did not care how my guys graduated with their GEDs. It was their day, not mine. It was only that we had been entirely disregarded in the event, a tendency in one degree or another that has been unfortunately present since the beginning of my employment, truly. So when it came to retiring, I went out a winner. As far as I was concerned, someone else could handle the craziness.

The Teacher and Inmate Discipline

D iscipline in the prison system and the governing rules are not the same as in a regular school setting. In general, rules and the consequences of breaking them should be clear and specific. In addition, they should be communicated to all concerned: the teachers, managers, and others. In the district, all prison institutions use Title 15 as the basic "bible" that directs the day-to-day action in the prison. Any inmate who knows his salt will know this book backward and forward. Teachers need to understand it in the areas that are covered in the classroom.

On page 14, this "bible" says, "The procedures established by the director, Warden Superintendent and Parole Region, are responsible for the operation of that receptive authority." Section 3005 (a) says, "Inmates shall obey all laws and regulations and refrain from behavior which might lead to violence, disorder, or otherwise endanger faculty, outside community or other persons." All in all, it's pretty straightforward.

As teachers, we know that the institution is like sitting on a powder keg. It can be quiet 95 percent of the time; it's the last 5 percent that can become explosive. We must always be alert, and every teacher must have a working knowledge of two key Title 15 sections that pertain to discipline. Furthermore, they must know how to write up these violations in such a way that they will not be dismissed or written wrong. The sections for us that I shall describe are Participation 3040 (a) and Performance 3641. Those are the two key parts for us to use so that we can carry out our duties.

Under the first one, Participation 3040 (a), "Every able bodied inmate is subject to an obligation to work as assigned by staff and personnel." This will be a full day of work or of education. These inmates are processed by classification, including yard captain, psychologist, counselor, and sometimes, a teacher. This inmate placemat is really made with (a) inmate approval or (b) the teacher's approval. On paper, the concept isn't too terrible. But in execution, it is yet another way that managerial efforts "put round pegs into square holes." Never during the process are teachers asked for their input, and even when we are, it doesn't go very far, acting only as a lip service. Once the placements have been complete, it takes an act of God to reserve it. Such an example is when an inmate is assigned to me and he has a GED or high school diploma, it can take about six months before I can have him removed to somewhere else. Now I have an inmate upset every day as to why he is in a GED class when he already has one. Now we have an unhappy camper who does not come to class, and I have to find out where he is because if he is not working me, I am still responsible for him and his actions. Therefore, even though the inmate does not want to be there and I do not want him there, the fickle finger of corrections has him placed there to make his/my life miserable. He is required to be in my class during certain parts of the day, and it not it will be written up. I must digress for a minute. When a write-up is given to an inmate who has 466 years to serve, it means nothing. The answer for the write-up is "So what."

The second section of Title 15 covers is performance. Performance 3041 is the code that gives us the ability to write disciplinary reports and, for clarity of purpose, is outlined below:

Performance 3041

a. Inmates must perform assigned tasks diligently and conscientiously. Inmates must not pretend illness, or otherwise evade attendance or avoid performance in assigned work, education and programs, or encourage others to do so.

b. Inmates must report to their place of assignment at the time designated by the institution's schedule of activities and as instructed by their assignment supervisor. (Instance: Inmates who are in education must be in the classroom at 0700).

c. Inmates assigned to education must cooperate with the teacher and may not leave the area without permission to do so (Instance: If an inmate needs to use the bathroom, he had to use the bathroom pass. So not only am I a teacher, I am a bathroom monitor. I am not about to tell a grown man of about 240 pounds who has slaughtered his whole family and given a life without parole that he cannot use the bathroom.

All these are rules that the inmates have to follow in the educational setting. An example of what a write-up looks like is below:

CDC NUMBER k65483
NAME: SMITH
BLDG: 5-213UP ON 6-21-201 I

As a GED teacher, I noted that 0721 Inmate Smith had not signed in and/or was not here. The building was called, and inmate Smith refused to attend class. He will be kept in his cell. This 128A will be placed in his file.

Inmate Smith is aware of this report.

Date: 6-21-201 I SMLOCKSHIN
GED TEACHER
C. Smith
Captain
Inmate File
Teacher Copy

Usually, an inmate would be given a verbal warning, by a 128A; then if that did not work, a 115.

Ample of the 115
CDC 115
CDC: K65483
NAME: SMITH

Inmate Smith received a 128A on 6-21-2011 and did not report to his job assignment on 6- 24-2011. The purpose of this test was to provide scores that would enable the teachers to search for weaknesses and, most of all, the students' strengths. Again and again the same issues occurred, which was all of these tests were constantly repeated. In other words, students would take the same test up to seven or at least eight times without any scores. As you can imagine, they became increasingly pissed off, taking the same thing over and over again. The students have been administered the tests themselves. An example of the testing day follows below:

06:30—Report to work.

06:45—Have the testing secretary provide the books and new Scantrons. The teacher then had to make sure that all the books were received, had all the pages, and that nothing had been written in them.

7:15—The teachers would then fill in the critical parts of the Scantron for the day's testing.

08:00—The students would come to the testing classroom and be checked off on a sheet. They would work on math/English tests as the teachers (usually two for twenty-four students) would go over the directions for the test.

08:20—Test begins.

10:20—Test ends. Make sure all books, answer sheets, pencils, and any scratch paper are collected before class is released.

11:45–1:45—Afternoon group. The same procedures applied as the morning group.

** There were additional problems with this program, and additional material is provided below.

1. What happened if there was an incident and the yard was locked down? The Scantrons would now be worthless. All the information on them would have to be erased and used at another date for another group.
2. Constant testing with no score/results not returned in a timely manner.
3. Teachers controlling inmates again over constant testing without results.
4. Constant bullying from management about scores when 98 percent of any errors were from poor communication.
5. Inmates who were released from prison retuned on a new sentence and had to start the program all over again.
6. Test scores returned when the inmate unassigned, transferred, or paroled.
   And most of all…
7. Sending files to other organizations when all you had was a name and nothing else in the folder. (This program ate up time like you would not believe.)

The only good thing that came out of this program was that we teachers would go to the inmates' cells and provide surveys on what they had achieved in school, such as grade level and their strength/weaknesses. We would provide material in all areas of study, make copies, take them to their cells, allow a few days for working on it, collect, grade, and then return to start the process all over again. We did this on our own to provide material and educational support that they were not getting under the Bridging Program. The major problem is that this program was the greatest failure that CDC ever had.

As a matter of fact, the problem went to Sacramento, and the *Californian Watch* wrote in March 2011 the following:

OFFICIALS TO OVERHAUL PRISON EDUCATION AMID COMPLAINTS

State officials are moving to revamp educational classes in prisons across California following complaints that the programs are poorly designed and could leave some inmates ill prepared for life after release. A draft last week by the California Rehabilitation Oversight Board cited ongoing problems including "increases in class size, reduced time in class, administrative paperwork, student turnover, wrongly assigned students, inmate homework, and elimination of vocational programs. In some California prisons, teachers are struggling to handle as many as 150 students while inmates get as little as three hours of classroom instruction per week. The report warned ineffective programs could hinder the rehabilitation of inmates. This, in turn, undermines efforts to reduce prison overcrowding by cutting recidivism.

Many problems arose last year after budget cuts led the Department of Corrections to develop five academic models and a literacy program that attempted to maximize enrollment by adjusting the number of hours inmates spend in class each week. The department also reduced the number of vocational classes by almost 75 %. Only keeping programs that are industry certified, market driven based on employment outlook data, have a minimum starting pay of $15 per hour and can be completed in 12 months.

The report by the rehabilitation oversight board found the new educational models did not comply with recommendations of a 2007 expert panel and were not 'evidenced based' programs.

Prison educators agree.

"It's a numbers game. It's not education," said John Kern, the Service Employees International Union Local 1000, which are enrolled in academic classes. Last year, many ended up in "Model 4," which has a target ratio of 120-1; approximately 82 % of the teachers [were assigned to it]. Programs said they spent most of their time managing paperwork instead of working with student according to union surveys. "The classroom resembled more of a train station than anything else, with the trains running slowly canceled. "Kern said.

Prison officials conceded that program cuts were aggressive and some education models were poorly implemented. "What we're receiving in feedback from teachers, students, administrators alike is that we are stretched too fat and that the teachers feel they have to see so many students now they really can't be effective at all," said Matthew Cite, Secretary of the California Department of Corrections and Rehabilitation. Cate said the department was working with educators and administrators to retool the academic models and cut the student teacher ratio to more manageable levels.

Ergo as the above article states, there have to be changes, as the idea of smoking mirrors has got to go. The goal is to have inmates properly assessed so that they are in the right class and the right program. Another part of the problem is that the last two missions that the State Legislature and CDC have tried were that of the Bridging Program of 54-1, and the second of having teachers working with a ratio of 120 to 1 (the program worked in this manner: twenty-four students a day, two sessions of twelve [the students came from three hours per week only]).

Both programs were wonderful failures for the following reasons:

Failure One

The students had to have mandatory TABE/CASAS testing. We administered these seven or eight times to each of the students only to get the scores very late. You can imagine the frustration from students and teachers. Both of us wanted the results. These were always weeks late, and the teachers bore the brunt of all the problems. We had office technicians who failed to do their job but were quick to blame us teachers for their defects. More time was spent by them in sending memos to the principal of higher authority than spent grading the material.

Failure Two

Many times, the students were locked down due to custody issues, and the teachers were not allowed to go to the housing units to leave material. Under the Bridging Program, we were to spend thirty minutes per week with each student. It never happened. It made no sense for us to be in the unit going over school material when the inmate was locked inside his cell and I on the other side with a door between us.

Failure Three

On the ratio of 120 to 1 after the Bridging fiasco, it was determined that we would minister, as mentioned above, to the students three hours per class per week. I complained that, as a GED teacher, it was never enough time to meet with them for three hours. They (the inmates) were expected to do homework in their cells for the next session. Imagine being in a cell one-by-seven feet, doing this with all the noise around you. The inmate was supposed to do this with, for example, his cell mate taking a dump. On top of this, the paperwork was just impossible.

Management expected all the paperwork to be done when the inmates were locked down. These complaints were ignored and went unanswered.

Failure Four

Under Bridging, we have to keep files on the 54-1 ratio, which was a joke in itself. The prison was an inmate assignment department, which places them at different tasks. They provide a DMA (Daily Movement Sheet), which tell all staff when the inmate assigned left an area, transferred, paroled medical, their bed moves, etc. The print-outs were so unreadable that we did not know who went where. For example:

> Name: Smith CDC #45688 Assigned 10-10-10
> 10-10-10 Assigned Orientation book issued
> 10-30-10 Unassigned

We kept file folders with this information, and when the course was completed, this information was to be sent to parole or the prison the inmate was sent to. Most of the time, all we had was a folder in it. Usually results from all the testing would come to us long after the inmate had transferred to wherever. And all we had was a mound of paper.

These two programs were a waste of time on our part, and smoking mirrors on the part of both the legislature and CDC. All it did was to waste the taxpayers' money for a program that went nowhere.

Strange Brew

J oseph Conrad wrote a wonderful book called *Heart of Darkness* (if he had lived today and worked at Lancaster State Prison, it would have had the title *Heart of Madness*). I couldn't stop writing, and while my friend edited, I kept writing "Strange Brew," some items I believe you find hard to handle, weird, and a waste of our tax dollars. So this is the very last and so I shall start:

Rip Van Winkle

A teacher, who worked in one of our vocational shops, had no students, slept in his office for five years, and then retired.

The Mad Hatter

An academic teacher who had worked in a state mental institution and needed mental health herself sat in a classroom for months on end, staring into space and telling her student she heard voices.

Mr. Electric

The electrical teacher who ran a class, taught students how to repair all devices like large floor fans and HP typewriters. Teachers would bring, for example, a large floor fan with one blade missing and got back a fan with no blades at all. The missing blades would be turned into wonderful knives for the inmate to produce. Typewriters would be sent to this seer of knowledge with a stick key, jammed return key, and get back a machine with no keys. He had told management he could repair copiers, so our department cancelled the repair contract to save on cost. The joke was on us. He had no clue how to repair them.

Robin Hood and His Merry Men

We had a classroom where the teacher didn't know his student made bows and arrows out of pencils and used the cork ceiling as a target. Management came into the class one day and saw the pencils in the ceiling.

Old Sleepy

Working in the prison when one is awake is tough, but much more so when one is asleep. I've had an academic teacher who would fall asleep in the classroom. I know this for a fact. I was acting supervisor when I went to check on a few classes and found him asleep with a class of inmates. His colleagues on either side of his room knew about this issue and ignored it. I suggested he seek medical attention than rather wake up with a slit throat.

The Queen of Hearts

Another manager was becoming the acting principal who created a reign of terror worse than the one from the French revolution. Every time teachers disagreed with her, it was like "off with their heads." At one staff meeting, she told us we could not eat our lunch while she chewed on a chicken leg. I told myself, "Well, shit to that." I started eating, and so did everyone else. She was like the plague until the warden had enough of her nonsense and removed her.

Fortress Teacher

This person started on the A Yard in the morning and moved to B Yard by the end of that day. In her classroom, she had placed filing cabinets all around her desk so that no student could approach her. There was a stack of boxes that allowed her to enter/leave from this walled area. She was totally inaccessible to staff and inmates. All she needed to make it complete was a moat and drawbridge. When the yard captain saw this fixture, it came down like the walls of Jericho, and she was transferred the same day.

The Hoarder

Over the years, we had a teacher who turned his classroom into a warehouse as well. Every year, teachers were allocated funds to buy books for their classes. And throughout the years, he had collected over two hundred boxes of material that he never opened. For years, it was rumored that he had ordered 25,000 pencils, just in case there was a pencil famine.

He also had an inmate trustee who would order this class's educational materials such as *The French Foreign Legion*, *I Bombed Pearl Harbor*, and many more titles that had nothing to do with education. We, the taxpayers, provided his own personal library.

The Invisible Man

The institution had substitute teachers who would fill in when other teachers were ill or went on vacation. We had one worthy fellow who was in this position. He would appear each morning at 6:00 a.m. and leave at 2:30 p.m., and no one knew where he disappeared to during the day. One would assume that management would know what assignment or classroom he was in—that would be too simple to deal with. Alas, not! He worked this gig for six years, until he retired, exhausted from this endeavor.

Mr. Vanity

The supervisor who came to work each day looked at himself in a four-inch-by-four-inch mirror all day. Adjusting his tie or moustache was more important than other tasks. He had to make sure he looked good.

Indeed, in the summer months when the temperature was 110 degrees in the shade and 106 degrees in the classroom, he would be crisp and cool thanks to air-conditioning. Our classrooms had swamp coolers, and with the humidity in the classrooms at 100 percent we cooked in our own juices. Our leader would call us and say, "Stan, are the inmates restless in this head?"

"No, all I can smell is the stink of twenty-seven rotting asses and feet! You should come to my class. It's awful!"

"I really would like to, but I've got to fix my tie."

He couldn't give a shit about what went on. Keeping up his vanity was more crucial to him.

The Greasy Spoon Sandwich Shop

The prison had two centers to get food: one legally and one not. Our "Greasy Spoon" was the unauthorized one. The legal one was operated by an outsider vendor that is purely operated by us.

Teachers on the E Yard had a trailer that was to be used as a group work station, which it was, but it was used for so much more. This enterprise was unauthorized and illegal, but used by many. How did it start? Well, I'll tell you!

We teachers didn't want to walk to the administration building to purchase goof. We took a vote to cook in the trailer. Most of us agreed that the snack bar was (1) too far, (2) too expensive, and (3) tasted like crap. So one of our teachers brought in two large hot plates. We could get water from our cooler or the restroom for cleanup. We all provided coffee, paper plates, and more for $15 a month. We operated from 6:00 a.m. to one in the morning. We would have ham and eggs, bacon and eggs, cheese and eggs, or anything else. And voilà! We were operational.

Of course this couldn't be kept quiet, and soon we had orders from teachers on other yards. We had orders for breakfast and lunch. "No good deed goes unpunished." Our popularity had grown to the point that everyone and their brother were calling in food orders. We had electric golf carts delivering food five to six hours a day.

The End of the Day

Well, it's almost over. Soon you won't need to read anymore. In truth, I have enjoyed teaching at Lancaster State Prison. I know I've complained enough about a lot, but my heart has always been about teaching here. I'm not a bleeding heart, and yes, the inmates are here for punishment, not as a punishment. No one comes to this place for three hot meals and a cot. And yet, they are still people. Society as always sent inmates to remote sites with the thought "out of sight, out of mind."

The incarcerated in the nineteenth century were sent to places where they could be with the rest of proper society, like Botany Bay Australia or Georgia. John Q. Public would use an iron hand to punish rather than find a methodology for change. Keep the inmate behind bars. The bottom line is that when the inmate is locked up for twenty to thirty years or life without parole, there may be some sort of change in the inmate. People can and do change, and even these are entitled to some sort of redemption or rehabilitation for release. We can't continue to use the same old method of "lock them up and throw away the key." It's just too damn expensive.

The modality of the inmate walking the yard day in and day out won't work forever. Programs that provide some sort of job training are more meaningful. Classes that will provide computer or electronic classes would be more beneficial. Get rid of the make-work programs such as twenty inmates sweeping the first from the exercise yard. Smarter people than I have asked the question "Who created the inmate?" Is it society or the individual? We see young children about the age of four or five, and they are innocent and pure. Now transport them fifteen years later, and this child is doing a twenty-to-life sentence and is tattooed from head to toe.

What happened to create this person? Is it a lack thereof? Family, no social structure—society's fault? I have a thousand questions and no answers.

I miss my students. On the very last day of class (8-10-12), we went through two boxes of Kleenex. An unbroken bond had been formed between them, and I was able to provide the services of education for them. A symbiotic relationship had been formed. They knew I was there to help, and they truly appreciated it. I have them in my thoughts. I do not miss the insanity and stupidity of nonfunctioning minds, not the endless lockdowns or searching, or the staff watching and playing video games and doing puzzles. Such a waste of taxpayer dollars.

I certainly have not missed the attitude of many officers and free staff who believed that education and educators were a waste of time and money. To those who did their job and were above board I say, "Stay true to your craft. You did and do a great job." This system of incarceration not only beats the inmates into the ground but also those who work there.

After all the years that I worked at the institution, my goal was never to be beaten myself. I came out with the same mental attitude that I came in with—all right, so I'm a little crazier than before, but that is all right. I can live with it.

I do miss the great managers and teachers that I have worked with, and you know who you are. You made a difference in this place and are worth your weight in gold. To those people I say, "Keep the flame of education burning strong."

So this is my story. It's taken over a decade to write, but it's been the labor of love I needed to get through the most difficult of days. My intent has never been to offend anyone, but to only use my experiences for this book as my contribution to progress. I'm just a small cog in the machine.

I'd like to thank my family and especially Rhona, my wife of over forty-five years, for being a great inspiration for me. Love ya, Beannate.

Thanks for the memories and the chance to write this.

Glossary Terms

A-B. Aryan Brotherhood.

Administrative segregation. Also known as "Ad-Seg," or "The Hole." An inmate is placed here usually for disciplinary problems. Inmates are in the cell for twenty-three to twenty-four hours a day.

All day. Inmate with a life sentence.

Bone crusher. A shank that's usually made from a stolen kitchen oven rod.

Border brothers. Mexican-American inmates' heavy gang ties.

Bunkie. Cell-mate.

C File. Contains history and criminal record of the inmate. Can be hundreds of papers and files, a ten-ream copy paper box.

Chester. Child molester inmates (low ring on the totem pole).

Contraband. Any material not issued by the Department of Corrections. Usually all illegal material from drugs to cell phones.

Count. Inmates' area is counted between seven and nine times per day. It's a form of tracking and knowing where inmates are 24-7. During the bed check counts, the officers want to make sure the same inmates are assigned to a specific cell.

Dis. Term for disrespect.

Drop a dime. To rat someone out.

Ducat. Internal inmate pass.

Emergency count. When adding up inmates and the count is off, all inmates are sent back to their cells to be counted and done within ten minutes. Once the correct count is made, a "count clear" is called over the PA system.

Fish. Anyone new in the institution.

General population. Inmates not in Ad-Seg, protective custody or the hospital.

House. Inmate's name for their cell.

Ink. Anything that is used to provide tattoos (i.e., ink pens, or cartridges from a typewriter).

Kite. A message dropped to the sergeant's office that something dangerous will happen in the yard.

Lifer or L-Wop. Inmate in prison for a life sentence.

Locked down. Inmate locked in a cell for a length of time: one day to one year.

Mule. Inmate who provides things for sale.

On the leg. Inmate who wants special privileges.

Shank. Homemade weapon made from anything.

Strapped. Inmate carrying a shank.

To be gassed. Usually Ad-Seg inmates who throw urine or feces at anyone walking by their cell.

About the Author

Chapter 1: Born in Brownsville, New York

I am Stan Lockshin, born in Brownsville, New York City, in the middle of a blizzard. It's true. On December 30, 1947, New York City had the worst snowstorm in fifty years. All my friends and family still think I caused the whiteout. In 518 Hopkinson Avenue, where my family and I stayed, there were many religious Jews. My family on my mother's side came from Minsk, Russia, and where she came from in 1941, the city fell to the German invaders. Within hours of the German occupation, forty thousand men and boys between the ages of fifteen and forty-five were assembled for "registration" under penalty of death, and after being held for five days, they were marched off to a nearby wood and shot. It was a preview of things to come. My father was a good man.

We lived in a building that was three stories with two apartments to a floor and fire escape ladders in the front and back of the building. Our apartment, which faced the street, had three rooms: a bedroom, kitchen, and living room.

Annie, who lived nearby, was a chef. She prepared all the catering at weddings and special events she was hired for. She could make animals out of chopped liver and tuna fish, items now made out of ice. Her coleslaw was incredible—large chunks of cabbage marinating in a vinegar-sugar base. I used to take rye bread and her coleslaw and make sandwiches out of them. One summer, her apartment was painted by Mr. Palle, a neighbor. To her, he did a crappy job, and she told everyone on the block. They bickered over this for months, and it came to a head on a hot Sunday afternoon. My father and uncles were watching a ball game on TV. I and everyone else from the building were sitting outside on the stoop when Mr. Palle walked by. Annie saw her opportunity to pounce on him over the paint job. In anger, he called her a "navkah," the word for "whore," in front of everyone. I started to get my father and uncles when she jumped up, ran down the six steps to the sidewalk, and caught Mr. Palle on the jaw with a left and right hook, which sent him reeling. He then went to find the neighborhood cop. He wanted her arrested, and it went like this:

"I want Annie arrested for beating me up!" shouted Mr. Palle.

"What did you say or do to have Annie beat you up?" questioned the cop.

"I called her a *navkah*."

"Forget it, and you're lucky I don't beat you up for calling her that."

Brownsville was a part of Brooklyn, New York. It was truly a melting pot of diverse races and nationalities. There were Irish Catholics, Jews, Italians, Blacks, Germans, Russians, the Polish, and the Gypsies. It was a miniature United Nations. For many of us, our neighborhood was our entire existence; that is, until I was fourteen. Being Jewish is not what you think. These days, most people don't say outlandish things out loud anymore, but I still remember and do know that racism and anti-Semitism still exist.

My world as a child was Hopkinson Avenue, Pitkin Avenue in those days in the 1950s and 1960s. Picture Ventura Boulevard in California. Pitkin was just like it. It was trendy and somewhat upscale. It had Jewish and Yiddish playhouses. Brownsville had sectors of Little Italy, Ireland, and mostly Eastern European Jews. Sutter Avenue was our supermarket, where you could find fresh everything, fruits and vegetables, and oh, the smell was divine. Let's not forget Harry the butcher, who would cut your meat up for you and his shop. Bang! Off went the chicken's head! RIP! Our came the feathers as they would be burned off on a larger burner. I'd remember he smoked cigars. When ash would fall from the burning roll, he'd laughingly say, "That won't be any extra charge."

In my youth, Jewish families kept traditions of religion and culture. Food is a major part of Passover, and certain preparations keep meals aligned with religious requirements. Jews eat no pork or shellfish products. Meat animals had to have a cloven hoof, chew its cud, and be slaughtered in a religious procedure with a rabbi attending. We had to have two sets of dinnerware: one for meat, the other used daily, and they could not be intermingled.

When my mother cooked meat, it had to be placed on the drain board, heavily salted so that the meat would be drained of blood, because blood would be considered as life and had to be cooked well done. So now we ate steak, a roast, and lamb chops as tough as shoe leather. It could have been used as such, especially if you had a hole in your shoe. Eggs also. If you broke open an egg and there was any blood in it, it, too, was thrown out. The first time I ate medium or rare meat was in the military and almost threw up. I've been corrupted since then. A medium rare steak is just fine.

Actually, I would say Jewish life was, and still is, about food, laws, relationships, and enrichment. Ours was no exception. My family's religious and cultural beliefs were heavily instilled by my Baba (Grandmother), whom lived directly above us in her apartment she purchased in 1926, and Annie Lockshin. Yiddish, the historical language of the Ashkenazi Jews prior to the Holocaust, was spoken by over ten million people; 85 percent of the Jews who died in the Holocaust were Yiddish speakers. My Baba came to America from Minsk with her five brothers. Devout Jews, they had left the "programs" of Tsarist Anti-Semitic Russia. She read three newspapers every day: the *New York Post*, a Yiddish paper, and the *New York Times*.

She was a "starker," not fat, but stout at about five feet ten inches. She was slow to anger, generous, a great cook, and had a wonderful sense of humor. She lived a long life and passed away at eighty-four in 1980. She was very religious. In the Jewish religion, the Sabbath "Shabbos" started Friday night at sundown and ended Saturday night. Observant Jews don't work on Shabbas, nor do they drive, use any handheld devices, or use the phone to turn on gas or answer the phone.

She would leave the pilot light on the stove for eating and the kitchen light for seeing. My father, Bill, worked on Saturday, and my mother, Hannah, and I would do the tasks on Shabbos that Baba couldn't. On Saturday, Baba and I could go down the block to HES (Hebrew Educational Society), which was not only our temple, but also the Hebrew school and Jewish Community Center.

I was a copycat. Baba drank prune juice and drank Maxwell House Coffee every day. On Saturdays, she would have both drinks. One day, I had double of both and found myself in the bathroom at temple during services. Saturday was a very religious day except that, after temple, we boys would play softball in the bank parking lot. This also was a tradition.

My great-uncle Zalman had a Bolsovich (Communist) and had thrown a bomb at the Tsar at a parade in Minsk in 1905!

I never knew my Zayde (grandfather). He died of a heart attack in 1944 before I was born.

I think about my father all the time, my mother as well. My aunt Lille died of the Spanish flu, which was an epidemic that killed off twenty-seven million people after World War I. My grandmother took the loss to her grave.

My father went to night high school and worked during the day. He played baseball in an AAA League under the name Bill Lock, since using his real Jewish name would have made him unable to play. He was drafted into the American Army in 1940 and served until the end of the war in Europe. He met my mother at a Jewish temple in November 1942. He landed D-Day, June 6, 1944, and was wounded in action December 14, 1944, right before the Battle of the Bulge. They married June 1945 when my father was told his combat days were over.

My mother's family traveled from Russia to Liverpool, England. My grandfather, Isaac Cohen, was a tailor and served in the British Army in the Jewish Legion, which was assigned to the Middle East. I have no remembrance of either grandparent on my mother's side. I do know that Liverpool was bombed very heavily during the war. With rationing, getting food was difficult. After my parents had me, my father would bring as much as he could in the way of food as he could. In 1940, the German Air Force bombed Liverpool over thirty days consistently. With the war over in 1945, my mother was now a war bride and came to American on the *Queen Mary* in 1946 to start a life with her husband.

As my parents settled on Hopkinson Avenue, my father went back to school on the GI Bill. He got his BA in history from NYU (New York University) and then his master's in history from Saint John's University. With millions of ex-GIs, finding work was difficult, especially if he wanted to be a teacher. He found employment with the post office as a mailman, which he did for thirty-six years. It wasn't the career he wanted, but he had a family to support. In 1947 he was paid $40 a week. Our rent was $30 a month, and that didn't go far.

In those days, he schlepped a leather mail bag over his shoulder and walked his route. He was bitten by dogs over thirty-seven times in his career. One of the dogs that bit him died. When my dad came home, I always asked him to play softball with us kids, and after a hard day, he always did so. Seven or eight of us kids and he would go to the park and play, with never enough to fill two teams, but always enough to play if right or left field were closed and we pitched to ourselves. After sixty years, I look at those games, and him, with fondness.

My parents made ends meet by working at a hall that did weddings, Bar Mitzvahs, and funerals. On Saturday and Sunday nights, they ran the hat check concession, would tend to the guests by helping them with their hats and overcoats. In return, the patrons were given a claims check at the end of the event to claim their goods. My parents got a small salary plus tips.

When I was very young, I was a bed wetter! A heinous crime it was. I can remember being told at six years old that I wet the bed at night. It was a humiliating experience for me. I would be brought to my family and asked if I had pissed the bed the previous night in front of my aunts and uncles. I would put a brave face and say yes or no. It was incredibly hurtful to me to have to divulge something so personal at such a young age.

My family would ask, "Did you wet the bed?"

If I didn't, I'd say, "No, I was a good boy."

If I did, I'd say, "I did. I'm sorry, it won't happen again."

But of course it did. I had to suffer their scrutiny for a while longer until I didn't have to wet the bed and could use the bathroom.

I was self-employed at seven years old. It's true. My parents would go on vacation to Miami Beach, and I would collect soda bottles, which were redeemed for two cents, or five cents, depending on the size. I would collect my cash and use the proceeds to buy some books. At this age, I had my first employee management dispute. A boy my age named David worked for me collecting bottles, but he was lazy, and I fired him. I had to deal with a giant shit storm. He complained to his mother. She told mine, and mine told me.

I always looked for ways to make money from an early age. From the age of ten to twelve, I walked dogs in the summer and shoveled snow in the winter and had my own fun money. I was like a miser. Every day I would count all my cans, hoping that, by some miracle, it would grow. One time, even though I would charge my dad 12 percent interest on the money he would on occasion borrow from me. I realized it wasn't ethical and only charged him 6 percent on money he borrowed.

When I was in my senior year of high school and worked for the *Viking Press*, a publisher of books, I worked in the mail room for $1 an hour. The most fascinating event for me is when I met Jackie Kennedy, since she was one of the senior editors at the publishing house even though she was the wife of President John Kennedy. She was very gracious and charming.

When I graduated high school and in my early college years, I worked at our neighborhood supermarket. Met Food, as it was called, was on Ralph Avenue. Basically, a large grocery store with a separate butcher shop. The owner, Sam, had come from Poland, and he and his wife had both survived being in a death camp. As a reminder of the experience, he had a number tattoos on his right wrist.

Sam was a character. Caustic and very cheap most of the time, had the shape of a bowling pin. He was so cheap that once, when the store had a fire and not a great deal of damage was gone, the insurance company paid him for damaged cans that were to be thrown away.

Instead, Sam sold the canned good as "fire sale" and made money from both ends. With Sam, slavery was not dead. If I could have paid him for working for him, he would have loved it.

My main job was to box up the orders and bring them to the customer's home. Thursday, Friday, and Saturday were our busiest days. I rode a Schwinn bike that had a high basket in front of the handlebars. Most of the food was boxed, not bagged, which made it easier.

Sometimes the homes or apartments were close to Met Food, and others were eight to ten blocks away. When I delivered groceries, I usually got twenty-five cents to fifty cents as tip. I would ask the customers if they had any soda bottles that could be sent back to the store. Small glass bottles were two cents; each quart five cents. I would make an extra fifteen to twenty cents on each delivery. My weekly tips averaged about $40, and weekly pay was $25—and remember, this was 1966. This was pretty good money when gas was nineteen cents, a pack of cigarettes twenty-five cents, and a quart of milk and a loaf of bread also a quarter.

My most interesting episode with Sam came during the winter. It had started to snow, and the road was very icy. I had to deliver two gross of eggs (three hundred) to the home economics class at the high school about two blocks from the store. I wanted to use the sled; Sam, the bike. He won. I got halfway across a four-lane road when I hit a patch of black ice. I went one way and the bike another, all three hundred eggs spewing everywhere and breaking on the pavement. Needlessly to say, Sam was upset.

Every week, Sam would fire and rehire me back before the weekend for one reason or another. As cheap as Sam was, he surprised me in May of 1967. The draft for the military was breathing down my neck, and during the Vietnam War, I had no school deferment that would exempt me from serving. So I reenlisted in the Air Force before the Army could get me. Sam gave me a hundred-dollar bill as a gift. I was just dumbfounded as he did this as a going-away gift with tears in his eyes. I thought he was sick.

The shortest job I ever had lasted one hour at seventeen. I took a job with the coroner's office. I was to help wash and clean the freshly dead. My first shift was from four to midnight. While walking down the aisle, one of the corpses sat up and groaned due to air in the lungs or rigor mortis. Immediately upon viewing this ghastly sight, my bladder let go, and I voided it into my pants. Needless to say, I quit after that experience.

Most of the jobs I had as an adult were in sales. The jobs looked like an alphabet soup: Professional Research INC (PRI), ADT Alarm Co., and Allied Protection Industry (API), which we called assholes protecting idiots. I sold alarm systems and armed guard and patrol services. I also moonlighted at night as a teacher for Sylvan Learning Center.

I can honestly say that in over fifty years of working, I was only fired once and laid off once. When I was fired, I saw it coming. I worked for three area managers who wanted to be district manager and their instructions to me changed by the hour. Working for them was like being in a merry-go-round. I didn't know if I was coming or going. The final straw was this. One day, they all wanted to meet me for lunch, and I knew I was going with the wind. When I met these three, I asked them when my last day was. They were caught by surprise. My last day would be April 30, and that time it was April 26. With this information, I did the next best thing. I went out on disability, which lasted for six months. They had almost given me a heart attack. I played them before they played me.

The second example is that of a company that was going down the drain. I had worked for Professional Research, a medical company, for twelve years and had been working my way up to assistant national sales manager. The parent company terminated most employees, but the president of our company whose brother was the CEO of the parent company was the only one who didn't go down the drain. He was totally amazed that he and only he survived. I was not surprised at all. After all, blood is thicker than water.

Humility is the mother of invention. Looking for gainful employment sucks the life out of you, and this humility gives one the ability to kiss them in the ass: some flunky that you have more skill and knowledge than but he's on the other side of the desk, waiting for you to leave so he can go to lunch or whatever. He has a job no matter how mundane. It also teaches great self-reflection when you're going from interview 1, which you've blown off, to interview 2, that which you have not yet started, trying to constantly feel up to do the best that you can.

At one time of my life, I decided that I needed a partner to work with. In hindsight, I should have passed on this mind fart and continued to work alone. I needed to be in business. It was just one pick in my bucket list that I should have passed on it.

To put it bluntly, have you ever worked with an individual for five years and not really know them? I was in that situation, where I was smarter than everyone else and no true progression happened. After I discovered that all the money we had made had gone through his nose as a whole lot of "blow." Even though our checkbook was at two anti one, he was able to forge my name quite nicely. The end of a partnership is like a marriage that has turned to shit. In a marriage, there may be money and property split up. In this case, what was I going to get, my partner's nose?

People in general are happy to see you fail because it makes their dull and boring lives that much more interesting. I had people say to me, "I knew your business would fail." I answered that it had done well for four years. It did not matter to them. Bottom line, I failed! And people are happy to share your suffering. By covering your unhappiness, theirs become less important. When this whole incident was over and many years have passed, people still believed I had failed. It's amazing what personal perception is always right on.

With the exception of my partnership, most of the companies that I worked for won trophies, plaques, and awards. A great many came with a monetary award. So even though they now collect dust on the wall in my den, they provided an additional benefit financially.

Chapter 2: Neighbors, Friends, and Spirituality

The friends of my youth are still my friends over sixty years later. Michele Banks (née Zoeback), Fred Goldstein, and his sister Ellen—

these were the siblings I never had. Even through time and distance, we are still there for each other. They, like my friends from the Air Force, are closer than blood.

I still consider Irv and Lizzie Zoeback, as well as Sam and Sarah Goldstein, my second set of parents. Even though these two couples have passed on, I reflect on them a great deal. My friends went to school together from their elementary years to junior high. Fred and Ellen—the same high school. The Zoebacks and Goldsteins lived next door to us, and were very dear friends of my parents.

Liz was born in Germany. She and her sister, being Jewish, left the country by boat on September 15, 1939, two days before World War II started. Her parents were to leave on the next boat. It never happened. They were just two of the six million Jews killed by the Germans during the war.

Liz and Lizzie were a second mother to me for many reasons. Two stand out. The first is easy! She made the best macaroni salad in the world! (My wife's is a close second.) The second is not so easy. Let me explain.

My mother would walk me to PS 175, the local grade school, and drop me off. My first grade teacher, Ms. Steiglizt, would brutalize me by calling me "slob personified" and other nasty names. So when I was dropped off, I would run back home before my mother could, go to Lizzie's apartment, and ask her to save me! My mother would call Lizzie and tell her I was at school. Lizzie would say, "He's here." Ms. Steiglizt disliked my mother because my mom was president of the Parent-Teacher's Organization. After a week or two of this nonsense, my mother told my teacher to quit picking on a six-year-old boy or she would knock Ms. Steiglizt's teeth out. She was like a lion and not going to have some old biddy pick on her son.

I used to drive Michele and her brother Mark, who passed away in 2006, crazy. Whenever I was in trouble, which was often, I would run to Lizzie's apartment and yell "Save me!" She and her husband Irving were great people. The other set of adoptive parents, Sam and Sarah Goldstein, were fine people. As I grew older while living in California, I always called the four of them on Jewish New Year and wished them a "Happy New Year." Before Sam died at the age of ninety-one in 2015, I had the pleasure to talk to him one last time.

Pinoche! What a card game. My father taught me to play at ten years old. For Jewish people, especially those from New York, it's like playing bridge in Beverly Hills. I played this game with my dad and three of my great-uncles, Zalman the bomb thrower, a lawyer, and Harry, who was not that successful. He owned a lumber yard and made the frame for Castro Couches. All of them smoked cigars wherever we played. No one knew the dangers of hand-hand smoking and no one cared. We played twice a week. The most someone could lose was about five of six dollars. But the arguments over who misplayed were fantastic. All of them were religious but extremely worldly. Mr. great-uncle Sheleyni was a general practice physician who made house calls, even on Saturday. His office was in one room of his house.

Sheleyni was the doctor who, when I was sixteen, discovered a cancerous lump in my lymph nodes in my right armpit. After his exam, he visited to reevaluate me. I remember it well. It was on a Thursday. My father went with me. The lump had grown, and he contacted two surgeons named Thayer (father and son) who would operate on me at Brooklyn Jewish Hospital. Surgery was Friday morning. My mother was a mess because her father, my grandfather, had died in England (1952) of a cancerous mass on his brain. My mother was a nervous mess.

The operation was a complete success. They got it all. No chemo or radiation was needed. Annie travels on the Sabbath by a cab (it's a taboo to drive on Saturday) and came to visit. She promised me a three-speed bike when I got well and kept it. The only discomfort I had was when it became very cold my scar tissue would throb. Not only were we devout and traditional Jews, I did prayers when I woke up for meals and when I went to bed. We had softball leagues to which I belonged at the Jewish Center. The Leagues would play all the time with the exception of Friday night, Saturday, and all the holidays such as Yorn Kippur. The Day of Atonement was our holiest day. I can remember one Sunday when we played a nightly religious team of students who were studying to be rabbis. It was my tum to bat, and the pitcher was slow.

Their catcher said, "*Varf* (throw) the ball already!"

Their pitcher said, "I will."

"*Varf* the fucking ball!"

Nice talk.

Our team would always pony up for a new softball. A quarter here, a dime there. There were times we'd hit the cover off the ball and all you'd have would be a wooden core and a bunch of string wrapped around the ball. We had little money for new balls, so we'd wrap the ball up in black tape, which doubled its weight, and now you had to not a softball, but a black cannonball.

I enjoyed being Jewish and all the traditions that went with it. The Friday night Shabbat dinners, Annie's chicken soup with boiled or roasted chicken, the gizzards and chicken feet in the pot, the entire horniness of it all.

My whole life I've been an avid reader. I can read four or five books at the same time and know where I am in all of them. I've always liked school and was in the glee club until I entered junior high school. I even had the singer's role in "South Pacific" and had to wear a tuxedo for that role.

In the sixth grade, I took a test, which I passed, which would allow me to do grades 7 to 9 in two years. This was an advance program where you did a year and a half of schoolwork in one year in the two-year program.

The middle school Cold and Marcus CPS 263 was only three blocks from our apartment. In middle school, I played softball as a pitcher or catcher on the school team. All of my friends were in this special education program, and there was a great idea of school work and homework. Not too much time was left over for social activity. School ended at 3:00 p.m., but my day wasn't done yet. I had to go to temple and had another hour of class to prepare me for my Bar Mitzvah (confirmation for boys at thirteen, girls at twelve).

I went to two high schools. The first was Thomas Jefferson, to which I went for a year.

The second was Samuel L. Tilden for my junior and senior year, which I graduated from in June 1964. We had a graduating class of eighteen hundred students—the largest in New York City!

The reason for going to two high schools was that with the first, I had to take a bus both ways. One day, my friend and I had seats in the back of the bus and some teenagers who belonged to a local gang beat us to a pulp because we had seats. I got home physically beaten and bloodied, and when my parents saw my condition, the decision was made that we should move.

We moved to 5703 Tilden Avenue in Flatbush, right across the street from Tilden High school. Our rent jumped from $30 a month to $130. My parents now had their own bedroom. We also had a front and rear porch. My parents paid the increase even though it was difficult. The area was great, and the high school was better still. This move was a strain on my parents' pocketbook, but they wanted me to be safe.

Alas, in high school I was a mediocre student. I had to have a tutor in geometry and French at $10 per hour. As much as I tried, I realized I was no great thinker. However, I had two great teachers. The first was Mr. Titlebaum who taught history. He kept students motivated and treated us as young adults. He was a true mentor. I worked with him on the high school yearbook, history club, and the school paper. The other teacher was Mr. Swartzkorf, who taught French with a thick German accent. He had this fetish of sucking his teeth after each third word and sounded like a snake was hissing at you. He was a terrible teacher with a great sense of humor. In his classes I learned very little but laughed a lot.

I received my letter playing handball, which would come in handy when I was a long-term substitute teacher in East and South Central Los Angeles (1973–1975). I taught a lot of boys gym classes. The students wanted to play handball with me for twenty-five cents a game. I became a handball hustler and would make an extra $10–15 a day, which supplemented my $39 sub money. The coaches would always ask if I hustled the PE students, and I always said, "No!"

I realized that when I graduated my grades were not great, so in June 1964, I could forget being a military officer at West Point or ever going to law school. So at sixteen, I went to Brooklyn College and took day evening classes. In high school I circled the drain. In college, I went down it.

I started at Brooklyn College in September of 1964. It was a glorious disaster! I was only sixteen and a half. The guidance counselor ill advised me. She had me take college biology with lab: six and a half units. Needless to say, I was over my head. Friends who were premed suggested I drop the course, which I did, and got an F. My first year of college, I was on academic probation. The more I studied, the worse I did. Vietnam was escalating, and the draft was in. By 1967, I saw the handwriting on the wall and joined the Air Force at nineteen in 1967.

After basic training I was sent to Clark Airborne in the Philippines for two years. Most young men looked for booze and broads, and I was no exception. I got tired of that and took college classes on base from the University of the Philippines.

Hard to believe that I succeeded in the class that I took on base with real professors. In the two years at Clark (1967–1969), I took twenty units and had a B average! I also had a letter from Brooklyn College that they would take and transfer all my classes, and didn't have to attend classes at night.

I returned from Southeast Asia in June 1969 and was stationed at Edwards AFB until honorably discharged in June 1971. I only had to work twenty-four hours on and had seventy-two hours off. This was a great duty, and I enrolled at Antelope Valley Junior College. I acquired additional units with an A average. I think I did well because I was no longer a kid at sixteen but a man over 21 and a SGT in the Air Force.

April 3, I 970, was a game changer in my life. I met the woman I was going to marry that December 19 (we're still happily married after more than forty-five years). Even though I was married, we lived off base in Reseda, California. Every fourth day I had to drive out to our military site in the Mojave Desert, a round trip of 250 miles.

Before being discharged, I contacted Brooklyn College to transfer back in. I was in shock when they told me that (1) I could transfer back but I would lose sixty accredited units and (2) I would have to go back to college at night. They had voided the written promise they had made me. I was very distraught since their original acceptance that they had offered me was now null and void. Happily, my wife had sent my entire transcript to San Fernando Valley College (now Cal State, Northridge), and they accepted all my courses. The best part was that it was day classes I would be taking rather than night ones. Some of the required history classes would be at night because they were offered then.

One of the finest teachers I had at CSUN was D. Helmut Haussler. He taught classes such as Hitler's Germany and Hitler's Third Reich. He was spellbinding. His family left Black Forest, Germany, to America in 1936. He served in the 101 Airborne Paratroop Divisions in military intelligence. His job was to interrogate captured German prisoners to get as much useful information from them. Being a native German, he knew all the mannerisms to help break down the wall between himself and them. He had taught at CSUM for many years.

After class, he and a few of my friends would go to Denny's for coffee and relive World War II. Grade-wise, he never gave anyone an A. I always got a B! I took him for my master's program as a mentor. He told me that he never gave me an A, and that twelve units of study with him, he would give me an A for all the units. He was good at his word.

Chapter 3: Work

In 1973, I had my BA in history and my teaching credentials (lifetime) in 1974. The only teaching job that were opening as long-term substitute teacher was in East and South Central Los Angeles for $39 per diem. I took the job. A year later I was looking for work.

The Los Angeles School District, in its ultimate wisdom, wanted a minority teacher in East/South Central areas. I was the wrong minority. I went from five days a week to one or two and then nothing. When not subbing, I was on a CETA program for military veterans. When not teaching, I worked for Los Angeles Parks and Recreation at Sherman Oaks Park. I had a great job. My duties were to use a cart and pick up dog crap, not an especially pleasant odor during the summer.

I came to a crossroads whereby being a long-term sub position came to an end. I was not the minority the district was looking for. With my wife pregnant and considering the fact we liked to eat every day, I soon found a job in sales.

My sales career lasted from 1974 to 1996 when I realized I wanted to go back to teaching. I was hesitant to make a move, and my wife asked me, as has been stated in the book, "What would you like to be when you grow up?" My answer my next teaching position was clear enough.

I had picked up a BA in history at Cal State Northridge and was going back to teaching. But where? The Antelope Valley Union High School District was offering $32,000 per year. Then I found out that the California Department of Corrections was starting their pay at $39,000! Do the math. The extra $7,000 made teaching in the system well worth it. It was the best choice I've ever made. Having no retirement plan in sales, working for the state provided funding for my tomorrows. In May 1996, my career began.

In 2006, I acquired a master's in educational administration from California University Bakersfield, which had an annex campus at Antelope Valley, JC. It was touch work. I was fifty-eight and going back to school. Classes in this program started on Fridays from 4:00 p.m. to 8:00 p.m., and Saturdays from 8:00 a.m. to 4:00 p.m. My overall GPA was 3.6. I was told I had made the dean's List, which mattered, but I was much more interested in being a vice principal in academic educations at the prison.

I had two wonderful mentors: Tom Magiel, principal of education at the prison, he was an exceptional help to me in these endeavors, and Mr. Gene Gadagos, who was an outstanding professor and teacher. Classes were difficult yet insightful, stimulating, and helpful. Once I received my MA, I did a turnaround and decided I'd rather stay a teacher than go into management.

I had previously mentioned that my first attempt at college at sixteen was a disaster. I started to blossom educationally when I went overseas, when I was older and somewhat wiser. When I started college at the age of twenty-three, I was married and much more mature. I did not belong to any college clubs or activities. I felt that, at twenty-three, I was five to six years older than the average college student, more worldly after four years in the Air Force, two of them in Southeast Asia. I never paid much attention to anti-Vietnam groups or activists. I had no time for this. This is not to say I was a hermit either. I had managed to make many friends of both sexes, but my wife and I were the only married couple we know.

I went to school with my GI bill money but worked at the Northridge Broadway. The original "Al Bundy" from "Married with Children" selling shoes to customers with crusty feet. Some life! School and feet.

Chapter 4: Trips as a Child

My earliest memories regarding trips with my parents were very enjoyable. The very first trip I can remember was 1954. I was seven. My father had a 1950 Hudson, and we planned to drive to Miami Beach, Florida. In those days, there were very few truck stops, and my parents kept a wide-mouth glass milk bottle inside so I could pee in it while they drove. Truly, very classy.

The car broke down in Bamberg, North Carolina. The town was truly at the bottom South. I had never seen black-only bathrooms or water fountains before. Being from Brooklyn, New York, it was quite an experience for me. Since we were Jewish, there was no bargain either, and we kept our ethnic roots of being Jewish to ourselves. Otherwise, we never could have obtained a room, food, or anything else. The car had died and couldn't be repaired, and so we had to take the Greyhound bus. The three of us and a one-hundred-pound watermelon. It had been given as a gift. The watermelon made the trip to Lantos where I gave it to the Greyhound ticket agent. We made it to Miami Beach in good order.

As a child, my parents and I have traveled the entire Eastern Seaboard: from Montreal, Canada, to Havana, Cuba. In 1957 Castro was just becoming popular there. My went to take us to a very popular café; however, traffic was heavy, and we didn't make it. The cafe was blown up as a result of this governmental change. We were lucky the heavy traffic saved our lives.

My uncle was a tailor and sold suits. When Castro came to power and the country became a Communist regime, my uncle set fire to his business so the communists wouldn't get it and fled to Miami with the clothes on his back. The invasion was a glorious disaster, a fiasco.

My uncle was very lucky that he was not killed or captured by communist troops. However, many of his closest friends were killed, tortured, or captured. Years passed, and I married my wife and went on trips to Mexico and the Caribbean. One of my bucket-list trips was going in March 2014 to Paris and London. As a history maven, I visited the American cemetery and was overwhelmed and in awe of the cost of American lives. Freedom always has a cost in flesh and in blood. Lest we forget the cost of being free.

London was beautiful and very clean. Paris was a very dirty city with more graffiti than Los Angeles. French men, I observed, peed against wall doors and glass windows. Very classy. In 1967, I took a great trip with all expenses paid for by Uncle Sam from 1967 to 1969. I spend a glorious two years in Southeast Asia. I was a goodwill ambassador for the United States Air Force, saving the world from the Asian communist peril. I carried a top-secret cryptographic clearance. Most of the two years were spent in the Philippines.

Can you imagine a virile nineteen-year-old that had the opportunity to lustfully enjoy sex? Okay, I got laid a lot, but I was always sexually careful. I always had condoms! More than sex, I took my USA tours and visited many wonderful venues like the opening of an American root beer cafe in the middle of Manila. As a history guru, I saw and went to many places involved in the World War II. For example, I took the walking tour of the Bataan Death March.

I made a few close friends who I am still in contact with almost fifty years later—James Roose, Al Lindenfelser (who married my wife's best friend), Don Willard, and Norris Stevens. We were the Band of Brothers. I was and am closer to these people than anyone else in my life. My military experiences were worth a million dollars. We were and are closer than brothers.

I returned back to the Good USA and had asked to be sorted to base on the East Coast as I was a New Yorker. Makes sense, yes? Wrong! I wound up in California at the Thirty-Third Squadron, assigned at March AF13 Ca. Wait, there's more. I was working at Edwards AFB California, and at a site called Howe's Radio Relay. It was heaven. I worked a twenty-four-hour shift and was off seventy-two hours, so I worked one day out of four.

I can honestly say that, in my last two years of service (1969–1971), I didn't make any friends in this unit of only fifty-two men. I was friendly and sociable, and that was it. Maybe I did this because I had made all the friends I needed or wanted when I was overseas.

One of the things I mostly remember about being overseas was that the food was utter crap! In two years (1967–1969), I only had six meals that were great: the two Thanksgivings, Christmases, and Easters. A good deal of our pay went for food, either in the snack bars or the club. I also ate off base. We were warned not to eat produce because human crap was used for fertilizer and told we "get the shits" if we did. I got the shits eating in the mess hall!

The company that my mother worked for had its textile plant in Manila. The plant foreman invited me to spend a few days there with his family there. He was very hospitable to me and asked me if I could do a favor. He wanted me to go to the base bank and cash in a few pesos for dollars.

"How many pesos are there to a dollar?" I asked.

"Fifty thousand pesos." He lied. At the time, it was four pesos to the dollar.

"That turns out to be 12,500 USD," I replied. "I only made $140 a month. I could just see myself doing this at the base bank, and then sent to a prison for dealing at the black market."

Needless to say, I didn't cash his pesos, nor did I go to prison for fifteen years.

Office of Civil Rights

CERTIFICATE OF COMPLETION

THIS CERTIFICATE ACKNOWLEDGES THAT

STANLEY LOCKS

HAS SUCCESSFULLY COMPLETED

OCTOBER 7, 2005

EEO COUNSELOR TRAINING

CA DEPARTMENT OF CORRECTIONS
AND REHABILITATION

10 /7/05

BONITA KWONG
DATE

This is to certify that

Stan Lockshin

Has satisfactorily completed

VITAL ISSUES PROJECTS
FACILITATOR'S TRAINING

And is hereby deemed Proficient
And is Authorized to Facilitate

PERSONAL DEVELOPMENT LIFE MANAGEMENT
COGNITIVE BEHAVIORAL THERAPEUTIC
LIVING SKILLS PROGRAM

Dated this 19th Day of November 2004

C.E.O. Vital Issues Projects, Inc.

President, Vital Issues Projects, Inc.

Certificate
of
Appreciation

Appreciation is hereby expressed to

S. Lockshin

for your deligent efforts on behalf of the
Facility Wide TABE Testing.

Thank you for a job well done!!

California State Prison, Los Angeles County
Lancaster, California

Dr.

H. Merten, Supervisor of Academic Instruction (A)

K. Bradstreet, Supervisor of Vocational Instruction

October 7, 2004

Distinguished Teamwork Service

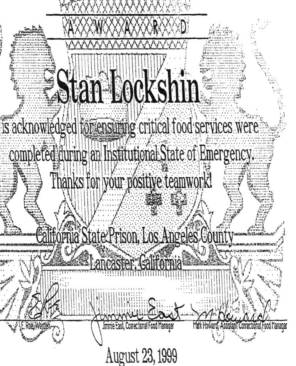

AWARD

Stan Lockshin

is acknowledged for ensuring critical food services were completed during an Institutional State of Emergency. Thanks for your positive teamwork!

California State Prison, Los Angeles County
Lancaster, California

E. Roe, Warden   Jimmie East, Correctional Food Manager   Mark Howard, Assistant Correctional Food Manager

August 23, 1999

State of California
Memorandum

Date: January 6, 1996
To: S. Lockshin
Academic Teacher

Subject: LETTER OF RECOGNITION

On January 6, 1999, you participated in the "1999 Quarter Break Training Program" and demonstrated a high level of initiative. You were assigned the task of Luncheon Clean-up. You demonstrated a strong personal commitment to successfully completing our training program project. I applaud your efforts to achieve optimal levels of personal performance and accomplishment.

As a result, our training day program was an overwhelming success and was appreciated by all Education Staff.

Thank you so much for your efforts and support.

L. Jackson
Supervisor of Vocational Education Program (A)

APPROVED TO BE PLACED IN PERSONNEL FILE:

The Last Class

Today is the last day of class, and boy, have I learned a lot in this class. So let me share a couple things with you. When I first moved, I didn't think I would learn anything from this class because I never had nobody really take time to teach me anything, but then came a man name Lockshin that loves to teach and loves to help people. He had a good man around. I learned a lot from him like math, people skills, how to shoot dogs—LOL. Just play hot. I will miss you and all your great stories. Lockshin, have a good life.

My Reflections on Mr. Lock's Class

I must say that even though I should not be here, I have enjoyed this class. Mainly, the reason is Mr. Lock; only when he is here in class though. His substitute teachers suck. Even though I have a high school education and a year and a half of college, I still enjoyed being in his class. Now that he is leaving, I do not want to be at ABE III.

When I first got here, I refused to do any work, but after I got to know Mr. Lock, I started to do work and help others. I learned patience and listened to other people's own ideas. I made some new friends and learned to help other people and not just myself.

Another lesson is that Mr. Lock gives paper, folders, pen, and brings movies for us to watch. He cares about his students and try with all his heart to help the students learn what they need. Even though my writing sucks, he seems to understand. He will be sadly missed here. He is the only teacher here at Cansaster that I like, admire, and respect.

Date: August 9, 2012
To: Whom It May Concern
From: Leda Medearis, Principal

Subject: Stanley Lockshin

It is my pleasure to write this letter of recommendation for Mr. Stanley Lockshin. As a teacher, he has been employed at the California Department of Corrections and Rehabilitation (Los Angeles County LAC) for over sixteen years. As the principal, I arrived in January 2012 to LAC. Previously, I was the principal at Juvenile Justice in Norwalk, California, and had the highest rate of graduation of all of the Division of Juvenile Justice Schools.

Knowing how important that good schools are made by good teachers, Mr. Lockshin is a dedicated, resourceful teacher. He totally engages the students in higher learning process. I can always count on him to meet or exceed expectations in the area of education. Mr. Lockshin teaches the GED program, and it has been very successful for our school. We just had a graduation, and the students congratulated Mr. Lockshin for all his hard work with the students in achieving and realizing their goals for education.

In addition to teaching duties, Mr. Lockshin has served on a number of advisory committees, such as the WASC Accreditation Committee and the Faculty Advisory Committee.

Mr. Lockshin would a valuable addition to any faculty or organization. He has a strong work ethic and keenness of mind. His willingness to take on new challenges makes him an exemplary employee in any future endeavor.

Mrs. Leda Medearis, Principal
661–729–2000 x 7692

The Last Class

There is a saying that God's all good things must come to an end. And alas, my friend, we seem to be reaching that point.

Our association for this many years has been a very happy one and also very productive. I would be lying if I were to say anything other than that I'll miss you, old friend. Our conversations, the seemingly mindless trivia we share and most of all the times we confided in each other about life's trials and tribulations. Its ups and downs. I don't think I've ever had a teacher quite like you! (smiles) Another one... you're one of a kind.

Oh, yeah, we can't forget about the towns where the donkey rules! (smiles)

Yes, my friend, it's a sad thing, but I'm sure you'll come by and check us out every now and then. You have been a bright shot. God bless you and your family always.

Your student and friend

My Reflection in ABE III

In the last three years I've been in this class, I've developed tremendously in math, reading, writing, history, English life skills. I have learned a lot from you, Lock, you're going to be missed.

You been the best teacher I have ever had to help me learn to develop some of these skills I need to become a better person. Lock, you have been here for each one of your students no matter what.

Thank you tremendously, very much for helping me to become a better person. I've learned a lot, Lock. I will personally miss you. God bless you, and your family. Take care of yourself. I hope to see you again. If you ever come back to this yard, I would love to come back to your class.

Good luck, stay strong.

Robinson

My relations _____ and _____ learn can be explain in a few words, like that each other classmate shown to one another. No matter what a classmate may be going through, there is always someone you can talk with. I learn there are great teachers, a teacher who loves to teach and see their student achieve their goals. That teacher have great respect among men. There no gift that can be given to show the greatness between student and teacher. I know student under that kind of teaching will be truely missed. This is a learning experince we would never forget. It was nice being in the class. My last words. This class is the "_iel for the soul"

152

Reflections.

It has been said by many. That school is a place of learning, social development, and achievement. As a youth I found many reasons to avoid going to class. Most profoundly, because of my lack of confidence.

I placed more value on playing games at school and basketball on the yard. I would shoot up as early as 6 a.m. and through the day, live for the moment the bell rings for recess, lunch, and a fieldtrip. I didn't take learning seriously. By the time I reached high school, I had ditched most of my school hours behind the gym with friends, or at a friends house). I had managed to be passed from grade on to high school, without actually a passing grade. I often think about what my life would have become had I the average to face my feelings of inadequacy in class. I didn't ask for extra help and my teachers had not notice? I've always been disturbed by the thought. I do wish I had the kind of class I have today, I believe I would have avoided the pit-falls of prison. There is a genuine degree of help and understanding provided to every person who wants to better themselves academically.

But, I do wish I had the opportunity to take the G.E.D. test.

My class ABE III   where

Educational... I learned a lot that I had not   something
known before, ~~I did not have any problem with it,~~
and I appreciated for it. The class was easy-going
among students and teacher, as though we were
~~had~~ known many years. The teacher's opened mind,
Students had more ~~thought~~

~~free &~~ comfortable times for   by and
their companionship. ~~had a~~ Personally, ~~I~~ I had
a problem with ~~this~~ ~~no~~ uncontrollable noises,
and I ~~the~~ thought ~~for that~~ I'm in a flea
sometimes   and
~~a~~ market, why students bring in
a personal business and make ~~noise~~
unnecessary noise for ~~to~~ others students
That is not mature behavior at all!
However, I was ~~really~~ liked this class,
ABE III and teacher.

                              Mike
                              Quiel

3/2/96

AB3-006

THIS CLASS HAS BEEN A FIRST
AND IN MY FIRST TIME BEING
HERE I'VE HAD THE OPPORTUNITY
TO LEARN ALOT... IN THE PAST
I NEVER LIKED CLASS OR SCHOOL.
BUT MY WHOLE PERSPECTIVE
HAS CHANGED. WHEN I FIRST GET
DUCKETED I ASKED TO BE LET
GO OUT OF THIS CLASS. WHEN
GOOD O-ME. LOCK HAD A TALK WITH
ME AND ASKED ME TO GIVE HIM A
CHANCE TO CHANGE MY VIEW ON
SCHOOL AND LEARNING - WELL IN ALL
OF THAT HE DID ALL HE SAYS HE
WOULD DO AND HE MADE LEARNING
FUN!! IN CLOSING I JUST WANT
TO SAY I COULDN'T OF ASKED
FOR A BETTER TEACHER AND
YOU MR. LOCK ARE REALLY A
GENTLEMAN AND A SCOLER AND
WE'LL REALLY MISS YOU.
        THANK YOU FOR YOUR
    KINDNESS. AND MY OUT
        BLESS YOU WHEREVER
    YOU GO.
        SINCERELY YOURS
            SINCERELY
            MR. CHARY
            ABRED:

155

My Class ABE III

I learned a lot something that I had not
known before, and I appreciated for it. The
class was easy-going among students and teacher
as though we were known many years.

However, because the teacher's agreed mind,
students had more free and comfortable time
for their conversation, so I had a hard time with
their uncomfortable noises sometimes.

The place where I came from, students or
work should be quiet and should be studied. Even
in prisons, I mean, prisons are more distinct

"The last Class".   3/29/04

Please write your reflections in this Class:

(1) What did you learn?
Where do I begin? Here in this Particular Class (with Mr. Lockshin), what he makes available for the Student who wishes to learn Academics, is (beyond measure.) There's an Old Cliche, that Says, "food is good, But when you cook with love, it becomes "Soul food". ☺
Well, that's our Mr. Lockshin. He teaches (us) with academics and Plenty of love. The man gives of Himself.

And for those of us in here who are Not merely Mature, but who (also) has an acknowledged desire to meet his fellow man to that Some degree, Mr. Lockshin is a breath of fresh air. So, in total, the C.D.C. hired Education instructor, Named Mr. Lockshin,

I S The Man!

Mr. Sudly James
P. 92656#

Iman-Umar (ibn) Tariq Aquil

157

"The Last Class"   Stev

What can I say about the "Last Class"? Wh
I came to this class, I had reservations. I don't do very w
in classroom settings. I struggle with sitting still and focusi
on school work. I came here with misconceptions that this cla
would be just like others, a waste of my time. In the past, o
few teachers have had anything to teach me that I cou
learn myself. I typically ignore information that doesn't int
me. After a short time in this class, I found myself in a rare
situation.

I met a portly teacher named Stan Lockshi
How different from most he was. It seemed to me th
he had a genuine concern with people learning about
things they didn't know. He taught us about things tha
we didn't know we wanted to learn! For the first ti
I found myself interested in school. I'm usually only interest
in stuff that teaches me how to do things, not about things

I've learned about history, literature, poli
and math. I've learned that the stuff that I do kno
isn't all I'm interested in. I've learned that people not
neccesarily intelligent as myself or other people, have things
to teach, even though they may not know it. Sometimes, the
smartest people learn that they don't know everything. I've
found that the most unlikely can learn. It takes a special
person to accomplish these things. Stan Lockshin is a spec
person. He has given us a reprieve from prison life by
having us interested in learning. It's hard to believe th
a teacher so good at teaching would be taken from his
students. How lucky the guys are that he will be teach
I envy them so. Over the passage of time, I hope that I
meet more teachers like Stan Lockshin! I doubt it.
        Thank you Stan!!!

                            Sincerely,
                              Mike Li

158

Jane. 8·9-12

1) write about what you've learned in this class?
2) what you thought of me as your teacher / Lockshin

1) I have learnd that no matter how much we Learn to better our
selfs, it wont do any good if we cant test what we learnd.

2) when i think about our teacher Lockshin, I see some one thats very
open minded, in with the understanding to get People like us, to
see the better Parts of how to Learn without makin things to hard
on ourself.

159

Lockshim?

What a beautiful teacher?
He is a teacher as milk
He gives us energy in my bo[dy]
and soul? The United States prod[uce]
about 900 million teachers
Lockshim is best of best teacher

He gave us information about
Social and Saul?

We need more program must be
Completed successful and satisf[i]
ation

Our jesus Will be give him
more happy life and heavier
and either life?

I am happy that our jesus
with him and me?

I don't know that will happen
Tomorrow but I expected
him Our jesus good than
very Well?? Thank you
Lockshim

Henry Williams

There is a technique in learning and a technique in teaching. Keeping a students interest is important so mixing entertainment along with education is essential in todays day and age. Lets look at technology for instance. Chalk boards and desk have been replaced with virtual online teachers and chat live rooms on specific subjects breaks the barriers of adament debators.

Scholars say that there is never a wrong question. I agree because everyone has a different degree of understanding. A different perspective and a way of processing things. A effective teacher can bring understanding to all.

Henry Williams

"THE LAST CLASS"

Question: What have I learn in Mr. Lockshin, class and what I think of him as a teacher.

Answer:

Mr. Lockshin, has taught me how to learn all over again. He have shown me that know matter what age one reaches, one still can learn what ever he put his mind too.

My opinion of Mr. Lockshin, is that he is the best teacher sense grade school. he has taught me more within a few months than that of my stay in the CDCR todate.

162

S tan Lockshin was lucky to have two careers: one in sales, for twenty-five years, and the other in education for eighteen. In his first career, he won many sales awards, causing a substantial sense of personal accomplishment in its very own right. And yet, it was the second career teaching at a state prison that proved to be more satisfying and rewarding.

Lockshin taught the GED program at Lancaster State Prison, a maximum security facility in the Antelope Valley, California. There, he managed a very successful program. The average percentage of students who passed the GED was about 80 percent. Furthermore, he served as vice principal numerous times and a senior member of the principal advisory group, and received many awards during his eighteen-year career.

He enjoys retirement and has been married to his wife, Rhona, for almost fifty years. His hobbies are target shooting and collecting World War II books. This is his first book.

CPSIA information can be obtained
at www.ICGtesting.com
Printed in the USA
BVHW091320260819
556817BV00014B/1285/P

He looked up and saw
a sunflower bright and yellow
in full bloom, and oh, so sweet!
smiling and waving hello.

Buzzy finally found a flower
to take some nectar home
What an interesting day! he thought,
Now, time to go back to the honeycomb.

He came back many a times
and did the flower-to-flower hop
it's a lot of work to make honey
but Buzzy will never stop!